In The Munitions
Women at War in Herefordshire

*In The Munition*s was first published in 2003 to celebrate the efforts of some of the women and men who had worked on the munitions at Rotherwas, Hereford through two World Wars.

Less than 300 of the estimated 6,000 workers are recorded on the Rotherwas Memorial on The Straight Mile. In this special reprint, coming a decade later, additional names of some of the workers have been recorded by their relatives.

As one relative, Rita Tabb put it: 'There should be something to remember all those who worked hard for their country.'

No medal of recognition has ever been awarded to the Munition Workers.

In The Munitions
Women at War in Herefordshire

Rotherwas munitions factory under construction during
the First World War, seen from Dinedor Hill

HEREFORDSHIRE LORE

www.herefordshire.org.uk

in association with

LOGASTON PRESS

Little Logaston, Logaston, Woonton, Almeley, Herefordshire HR3 6QH (www.logastonpress.co.uk)

First published by Herefordshire Lore & Logaston Press 2003
This edition published 2013
Copyright © text: Herefordshire Lore 2013
Copyright © illustrations as per Acknowledgments

ISBN 978 1873827 98 7

Set in Gill Sans and Baskerville by Logaston Press
and printed in Great Britain by
Bell & Bain Ltd., Glasgow

Cover illustration: Edith Davies from Railway Terrace, Stretton Sugwas, top left, seen here celebrating her birthday with friends in the 1940s, was badly affected by handling high explosives at the factory. She died not long after the war ended. (Photo: Graham Davies)

More than 50 women have helped to make this book. A
number of men have also contributed, but this is essentially
the story of the women who made munitions at the Royal
Ordnance Factory at Rotherwas. They tell their own stories
in their own words. This is their testimonial. At least 29 died
a violent death at the filling factory. Others died from the
effects of the explosives that they handled.
In The Munitions is dedicated to these women.

Editor: Bill Laws
Writer & Researcher: Bobbie Blackwell

Contents

Herefordshire Lore – Living Local History

Herefordshire Lore works to remember, celebrate and record Herefordshire's past before it is lost with the passing of generations. It is run by a group of volunteers, and can be reached on the internet at: www.herefordshirelore.org.uk.

The material for this book is based on the recollections of many older people. We are especially grateful to them and to all those who helped: Nellie & Francis Adams, Maud Andrews, John Bartle, Doreen Bell, John Billingham, Douglas Booton, Wilf Bowen, Mrs. T.J. Bowen, Marie Brightmore, Doris Brommage, Gwen Caldicutt, Dennis Chambers, Joan Clark, Bob Colley, Siniol Collins, Mary Compton, Patricia Cooper, Ella Davies, Evelyn Davies, Mr. A. Double, Jean Dubourg, Ada Eacock, John Edmonds, Grace Edmonds, Marjorie Edwards, M.E. Fabian, Nora Foster, Queenie Frears, Mrs. K.M. Gamble, Fred Griffiths, Joan Hiles, Hilda Holley, Sue Hubbard, Ken Hursey, Ken Hyett, Doreen Jackson, Irene Jones, Kathleen Jones, P.J. Jones, Eleanor Keates, Sidney Keates, Keith Lane, Nellie Latusek, David Lewis, John Lewis, Joyce Lewis, Rosemary Lillico, Eve Litchfield, Griff Lloyd, David Lovelace, Catherine McCann, James Markham, Violet Maysey, Molly Meyrick, Mary Morgan, Sybil Nicholls, Elizabeth Semper O'Keefe, Annie Pitman, Marjorie Powell, Priscilla Robbins, Stephanie Ross, Mrs. C.J. Sawdon, Richard Shaw, C.E. Shutt, Annie Slade, Hilda Skerrett, Brian Stevens, Brian Thomas, Hilda Tippings, Toby Tobijanski, Thelma Verhulst, Betty Watkins, Iris Watkins, Trevor Watkins, Adelaide Weekes, Derek Whittaker, Marion Willavoys, Dryslwyn Williams, Lenora Williams, Margaret Williams, Mrs. E. Winders, Michael and Doreen Wood, Margaret Woodward, Michael Young.

For pictures thanks are extended to Bobbie Blackwell, Dan Brown, Katie Causer, Molly & George Coleman, Jean Duborg, Norah Foster, Halcrow, *Hereford Times*, Herefordshire Libraries, Joan Hiles, Ken Hursey, Colin Keates, Joyce Lewis, Eve Lichfield, Mrs. A. Lynes, Philip Propert, Hilda Tipping, Sandra Watson, Chris Webb, Ken Webb, Connie Williams, and for the cover design: Chris White.

Our thanks too to the Herefordshire Lore team, especially our interviewers and Margaret Beare, Bobbie Blackwell, Mary Blackwell, Les Causer, Tamsyn Clayton, Anna Falcini, Vicky Hobson, Eileen Klotz, Harvey Payne, Sylvie Smith, Dawn Turner, John Turner.

This is a Local Heritage Initiative project which is a partnership between the Heritage Lottery Fund, Nationwide Building Society and the Countryside Agency.

Local Heritage *initiative*

Introduction

The Royal Ordnance Factory at Rotherwas, Hereford, employed nearly 4,000 women in the First World War. In the Second World War around 2,000 women worked there. *In The Munitions* is their testimonial.

Compiled from interviews with former workers, and presented as told, *In The Munitions* is a diary of the days when bombs, shells, landmines, torpedoes and weapons of modest, if not mass, destruction were made at the factory.

In The Munitions marks a moment in British history when women coped with adversity inside and outside the factory: childbirth and child care; absent fathers and amorous Americans; twelve hour shifts and dubious medical checks; sabotage and sickness; hardship and humour.

ROF Rotherwas. Former munitions worker Hilda Tipping's badge

Women on the munitions slipped notes in with the armaments 'so the soldiers knew we were thinking of them'. They found themselves on the receiving end of bombs: 'A girder struck my leg. I thought: I'll never get out of here. This is my lot'. And sometimes they feared the worst: 'My aunt said: "We're going to work tonight and I'm not coming home tomorrow". She never came home'.

'The plane was coming directly up the line of sheds towards me. The bomb bay was open and then I saw the bombs come out.'

'I was waiting on the Gate with my boy in my arms, worried. My husband was on nights and hadn't come home. "Haven't you heard? A bomb's been dropped on Rotherwas".'

In The Munitions provides a telling picture of times past. It also echoes the experiences of people caught up in contemporary conflicts — Chechnya, Kuwait, Palestine, Croatia, Bosnia, Iraq.

Annie Hall celebrated her hundredth birthday as *In The Munitions* went to press. Annie, almost certainly the last surviving worker from the First World War, went to work at Rotherwas when she was 16. 'They're looking for another war now', she remarked in March 2003. 'Terrible 'en it?'

Bill Laws, April 2003

Foreword

This book is the culmination of so much hard work by so many people. It tells the story of the experiences of some of the men and women who worked at the Royal Ordnance Factory at Rotherwas during both World Wars. This in itself is reason enough to publish it, but we must remember it directly records the voices and experiences of those that were there at the time. As such we find that some of the tales published here are amusing, sad and, for some, tragic, but all of them form an important part of Hereford's local history, a part which will become harder to reach as time marches on.

I would like to thank those whose efforts have made this book possible. The interviewees, interviewers and transcribers in particular need a mention. Without them this project and book would not have been the success it is. Bill Laws needs singular thanks for editing all the material into such an interesting and accessible read and finally I would like to acknowledge the financial support the project has received via the Local Heritage Initiative which is a partnership between the Heritage Lottery Fund, Nationwide Building Society and the Countryside Agency.

This book embodies all that Herefordshire Lore aims to achieve: recording the living memories so important to our local history and presenting them in an accessible way — really living Local History. I do hope you enjoy it.

John S. Turner
Chairman
Herefordshire Lore

First World War munitions workers pose for their picture on a nearby railway bridge

Rotherwas — From Catholicism to Munitions

Rotherwas house and its 2,577 acre estate date back to the 1450s. The original black and white building stood near a lane that wandered past Lower Bullingham following the riverbank before turning west to Dinedor Hill where it joined the straight mile at Sink Farm.

The estate, one of many belonging to the De La Barre family, was probably acquired during Norman incursions into Wales after 1066. Rotherwas came to the Bodenham family through the marriage of Sir Roger Bodenham to Isabella, heiress and only daughter of Walter de la Barre of Barres Court of Herefordshire.

The Bodenhams, descendants of the Lord of Monnington, were gentry associated with the parish of Bodenham in north Hereford. Through this marriage they also acquired large estates in the parishes of Kilpeck, Dewchurch and Tarrington. Another Sir Roger Bodenham, born in 1545, and his wife, Joan Brownieh, were the first to live at Rotherwas in 1583.

After the reformation in 1547 the Bodenhams, like many rich influential Catholic families, were finding it increasingly difficult to practise Catholicism openly. Some gave up and became Protestants. Others, like the Bodenhams, compromised their religious beliefs or practised in secret. Sir Roger, although a professed Protestant, had strong Catholic sympathies. Indeed his wife was a Catholic. In 1583 he built a domestic chapel on Rotherwas estate. The chapel may have been for his wife and servants — 'recusants' who refused to attend Protestant services, despite the risks. There is no record of the chapel, dedicated to St. Mary, having ever been consecrated, not surprisingly in view of the times. It saw both Catholic and Protestant use.

Sir Roger was knighted at the coronation of James I in 1603. King James II, described as the 'Wisest fool in Christendom', came to Rotherwas to visit Sir Roger with a large retinue of servants and hangers on. The King found Rotherwas a lovely place to be — so did all his followers who all wanted to stay. James sent most of them packing saying: 'You know, it is not given to all of us to dwell at Rotherwas'.

An engraving of Rotherwas House

Writing in 1597, Gerard, a Cheshire herbalist, compared Rotherwas to Kent, the Garden of England. It had so many apple trees that the servants drank nothing but cider. The pigs were so fussy they ate nothing but the best fallen fruits and the poor always had something in times of want 'to relieve their necessity'. The Wye was full of salmon.

Thomas succeeded Sir Roger, after his death from dropsy in 1623. Twenty years later, the Civil Wars of 1642-46 raged through Herefordshire between the Royalists and Roundheads, causing severe losses for the Bodenham estates.

The Scots Army sent two bailiffs and four musketeers to Rotherwas to plunder anything of value and soon the buildings had fallen derelict and the chapel lay unused for twenty years. However, family fortunes revived with the redistribution of seized lands during Charles II's reign. Hereford became a quiet, isolated backwater having lost its political importance as a strategic border defence town. Peace reigned more or less.

Until the 19th century, during Count Charles de la Barre Bodenham's time, roads in and out of Herefordshire were the worst in Britain. Amidst the quiet of the Rotherwas estate came a noise and clatter of large gangs of navvies, horses, carts and steam rollers, laying the Straight Mile to service the building of the Gloucester to Hereford railway with its four tunnels and four bridges, opened in 1855.

The new Rotherwas house was completed in 1865. Its owners, devout Catholics, founded two convents at Bullingham: an active order, the Sisters of Charity at Elizabeth's and a contemplative order, the Poor Clares at St. Raphael's. They also gave help to the poor of the area. The government's harsh Poor Law Amendment of 1834 removed parish responsibility for the poor, giving rise to the Workhouse. Count Charles died childless in 1883. His Polish wife died nine years later, to be succeeded by her nephew, Count Louis Bodenham Lubienski.

In 1907 a fire badly damaged the house and Count Lubienski spent his remaining years at Bullingham Manor. He died in 1909 leaving three children. It is believed the Count was virtually bankrupt.

Count Louis Bodenham Lubienski and his family inherited the Rotherwas Estate

The estate and house contents were auctioned in December 1912. An American oil magnate brought most of its Renaissance interior and superb furnishings for £70,000 and shipped them to Amherst College, Massachusetts, U.S.A. When the land was sold in 76 separate lots, the County Council brought 195 acres towards Bullingham. A Hereford businessman bought the lot that included the chapel planning to demolish the old buildings.

Count Lubienski's children sought the sanction of

the Home Office to have the bodies of their ancestors exhumed before they were desecrated. Thirty-nine bodies were exhumed from the chapel and reinterred in a private cemetery nearby, where the children's parents lay recently buried with other members of the Catholic community.

During the 1914-18 war Rotherwas House was used as a barracks for the military who guarded the munitions factory. The last service ever held at the chapel was in 1914. In 1926 Rotherwas House was demolished.

Mothballed. Blast walls and bunkers in 2003

Under construction. The National Shell Filling Factory being built at Rotherwas in 1915

The First World War

In the 1914-18 War, Zeppelin air raids threatened the safety of England's munitions factories. This, and a gross shortage of shells for our soldiers in France, was enough to persuade Lloyd George, then the Minister of Munitions, to increase weapons manufacture and to build 12 new munitions factories in remote areas of Britain. The government was on the lookout for open countryside, close to towns, with good rail communications, electricity and water supplies, and a large, local labour force.

The land around Rotherwas Manor, acquired by Hereford Council in 1912, fitted the bill perfectly. The Council sold the land to the Ministry of Munitions and the building of a new ordnance factory began on 11 July 1915. The plants were linked by 27 miles of standard gauge railway connected to the civilian Great Western Railway network. GWR staff were replaced with military operators before trains entered the site. There were ten miles of foot and sentry paths and three miles of roads surfaced with inert mastic to prevent static charges and reduce the risk of explosions during the transfer of munitions from one site to another.

There was an administration block, a 50-bed hospital and a separate power station and water supply. There was even a farm stocked with cattle to supply the canteens with fresh food and milk — by 1917 the nation had only six weeks supply of grain left. Rotherwas Manor was used as a barracks for the guards and the whole place was contained within nine miles of military guard fencing with security gates at each end of the Straight Mile.

Arms production began in November 1916, but in 1915 advertisements for workers had appeared in the *Hereford Times* with warnings that an insufficient response would lead to the need to invoke the Essential Workers Act.

The work was hard and dangerous. Women came from Leominster, Ludlow, Ross, South Wales and Birmingham. The first wave of outsiders found lodgings, but as numbers grew, tents and sheds were erected in the fields along Walnut Tree Avenue and Aylestone Hill to accommodate them. This new breed of working women, who still did not have the vote, made up two-thirds of the work force. The male war machine was, nevertheless, dependent on them.

Trains called 'Workgirl Specials' were laid on to bring them to their early and late shifts, but before beginning work they were strip-searched by male members of the military for matches and other contraband.

Lyddite, a poisonous, bitter yellow substance used in the production of explosives in the filling factory, caused toxic jaundice. Since they showed signs of jaundice earlier, dark-haired women were chosen for this job. Working with Lyddite and constantly stained yellow, these women were nicknamed 'the canaries'.

By 1917 the factory was producing 70,000 heavy shells a week — the young Winston Churchill aimed to supply the army in France with 66,000 tons of shells per week. Fifty pound and 230 pound aerial bombs, 'amatol block' charges and mustard gas chemical shells were being produced. By this date, 3,977 of the 5,940 employees at Rotherwas were women.

After the war the women went home. Rotherwas was used to break down ammunition and 400 men were employed until 1921. A skeleton staff stayed on and the buildings were used for army stores. In 1928 women got the vote on the same terms as men.

The Second World War
After the First World War only one munitions factory remained in production, but its proximity to London made it vulnerable to the emerging threat of modern air attack. Rotherwas, retained as an army storage depot since 1924 by the Ministry of War, was reactivated in 1932 as a small scale supplementary 'filling factory' to Woolwich.

Clandestine extension and modernisation programs began on the old factory in 1937 (later estimated to have cost £25 million). New buildings, railway sidings and track, locomotive

War workers. A recruitment drive at Castle Green, Hereford

repair sheds, 26 bomb filling sheds, 14 temporary Romney structures, 80 large air raid shelters, blast walls and earth banks were built. Three storage magazines, repair shops, offices, police huts, seven firemen's residential quarters, and in 1943 more Romney Huts and a pond were added. In January 1937, the manufacture of all military explosives was removed from Woolwich to Rotherwas.

As the importance of the factory gathered pace, so did the demand for labour. Accommodation for workers was a major concern for the Council, which in January 1939, established 9,124 'various rooms' within the city. Few, however, were near Rotherwas and it was not uncommon for whole families to occupy two rooms. One family of six even lived in a chicken shed for several weeks!

As some people criticised rearmament as a waste of money, others feared Hereford would become a prime target with a munitions factory so close to the city. Then, on 1 September 1939, war with Germany began.

By 1942 the war effort was absorbing over half the nation's income. Hereford's civilian population swelled with munition workers, land girls, members of the Women's Timber Corps, and evacuees. Existing accommodation was stretched to the limit and 'local' munitions workers travelled, some on bike, from as far afield as the Forest of Dean.

Hereford Council was desperate for more accommodation and in 1941 the Ministry of Supply financed the building of the Red Hill Hostel, off Mayberry Avenue. Managed by Holiday Fellowship Ltd., and described as a cross between a barracks and a Butlins, it could accommodate 2,000 people deployed on war work.

By 1940, Rotherwas employed over 5,000 workers. Of these, 700 male and 2,000 females earned the equivalent of £1.60 for a 47 hour week, filling naval mines, depth charges and torpedoes, 'hot' and 'cold' 25 pound shells, 250 pound and 2,000 pound bombs.

The factory suffered one serious air raid. At dawn on 27 July 1942, a German bomber dropped at least two 250kg bombs on the factory. The first hit a transit shed killing 19 people. The other struck a girder, was deflected through the shed door and ran out through the factory wire to hit the Police Superintendent's house, killing all but one of its occupants.

On 12 September 1941 a milling machine overheated, its volatile contents exploded and three workers were killed. George MacLaren, aged 28, and Francis Hicks, aged 45, died from severe injuries while Henry Charles Caleb Bigglestone, aged 42, was decapitated trying to bring the machine's safety hood down to protect other workers. Six others were hurt, but little damage was done to the factory.

This accident was overshadowed by what was later known as the 'Hereford Incident'. One Tuesday evening on 30 May 1944, Hereford was rocked by a massive explosion. Windows were smashed for miles around and people in cinemas — the city had several in those days — ran out fearing a blitz. Fire started in a South Section shed where workers were engaged in filling 2,000 pound bombs and naval mines. While the factories Assistant Fire Officer, F.A. Lewis, was arriving with a crew of five, an unsealed 2,000 pound bomb began smoking. An explosion was inevitable and evacuation began.

Process workers J.W. Little, F.J. Tyler and A.J. Morris stayed on, desperately trying to damp down the fire with water and sand until evacuation was complete. Thanks to them, 800 people reached safety. The Factory Fire Brigade took over, risking death from the fall of girders and molten explosives. Finally the bomb split open and exploded. Lewis and Leading Fireman W.J. Davies were hurled 30 feet out of the building. Knowing more bombs were burning, they returned to cool them with hoses, but a second, more powerful explosion sent sheets of flame 2,000 feet into the air. Mr. Lewis, crawling from under the rubble, took a man who had received severe facial injuries to the surgery before returning to the fire. Now, aided by the National Fire Services from four counties, they worked through the night. Process worker Vincent Carey was injured when the remaining bombs exploded. Men were thrown everywhere and one was killed. In addition Morris later died from injuries caused by his heroic deeds. As buildings collapsed, Carey, despite his injuries, pulled two men out from under the debris.

Even after the fires were extinguished 900 tons of live ammunition still lay under the wreckage and it took another month for a specialist team, headed by W.L. Fitzmaurice, to make the site safe. To protect his men, Fitzmaurice, under continuous hosepipe spray, defused 1,500 pounds of explosives on his own.

Later, at Buckingham Palace, King George V awarded five George Medals, nine British Empire Medals, an O.B.E. and an M.B.E. to the men for their bravery and endurance.

War ended in 1945 and Rotherwas, having being used for disarmament, finally closed in 1967. In 1985 its long history emerged again briefly when three First World War Picric Acid Stores and the possible remains of a medieval village were uncovered.

Bobbie Blackwell

My Name is Annie Slade

In 1915 Lloyd George, Minister for Munitions, directed that part of the old Rotherwas estate should be taken over from Herefordshire County Council and turned into an armaments factory, National Filling Factory No 14. The factory cost £200,000 to build and by the end of 1917 employed between 5,000 and 6,000 workers, most of them women.

One of them was Annie Slade. Born in 1903, Annie is thought to be the last surviving worker from the First World War:

Annie Slade,
First World War worker

My name is Annie Mary Slade and I was born in Pentre, Rhondda. My mother was from Aberystwyth and had come to the Rhondda to service.

We had a house on the side of the mountain and when I was eight years old we had a landslide. When I went up to bed all the furniture started shaking. The other house on the mountain went first. A friend of my mother had come to stay with her for a week with two little boys: I opened the bedroom door and half the house had gone and the little boys had gone with it. The men from the pit run up, and my mother run up, and they shouted on me to throw sheets out through the window. So I threw some sheets out. I threw my sister out first, the baby. And then I threw my other sister and I jumped out after. And then I went roaming the mountain. I didn't know where I was. The house went on fire in the end. We lost everything. My grandmother took us in until my mother had a house.

Then my father died when he was 40; he was a bit of a boss in the pit. He had a clout on top of his head but of course he never bothered about it and then in the end he had to go to the doctors. Well they touched something on his brain. He went blind, and then deaf. One nerve he had and that was his tooth nerve. We had to write on a slate if you wanted to tell him anything. I've still got the slate.

My mother would take washing in to keep us going. There was three girls and then my mother had two sons. My other sister, she died when she was 14½. She had heart trouble. So when I was 15½ I joined the army. We were stationed in Newport in the Westgate Hotel. There was a big room upstairs and they had all these sacks and then we had to run with the bayonets, you know, to the sacks. They said we ought to go to Cardiff to have a medical to go to France. So when they said we ought to go to France, me and my friend got on the train and went home! So the escorts come after us and they took us up the police station to question us. And they said: 'Well I'm sure she's under age'. So my mother come up and she fetched my birth certificate. So when they knew that we were under age they let us go.

I wanted to do something for my country. So then I joined the munition works, when I was 16. They sent me to Hereford, me and my friend. I lived first, for a year, with an old lady at Whitecross. Her friend used to make jelly and custard in little cups. Tuppence a cup. And me and my friend used to buy about half a dozen and we'd go down by the river to eat it.

Then I went to Ross-on-Wye after because it was nearer home in Wales. We'd go on the Work Girl Special train about 6.30 in the morning.

When I was in munitions' work I was on the Powder. The men were very polite to us, yes very polite. Nobody ever said a bad word to us. When you went in, you had to go through two barriers. One with your clothes on and you'd be searched. We were searched with our own clothes on and then when we went over the other barrier and we had to strip off and be searched in our underclothes. Women searched us. Then put all munition clothes on. And then we had pegs, all with our names, with our clothes hanging on 'em. And our munitions clothes was hung there when we finished. And then we were searched again going out. Yes, for fear we had any powder on us or anything. Taking it out with us!

They'd search you for any pins on you. You wore like a suit, yes, and these shoes, were soft. And we had like a hat and you had to tie it around your head. My uncle went to make shoes, but he was only there a couple of days because he had lovely, curly hair and his hair started going green. He left then.

There was surgery on the site as well, and dentists. Because, the powder, that's how I lost my teeth. I had lovely teeth, but the powder had gone into my gums.

And where I worked in the mills, where the powder was, you had to put TNT and AN [Amyl Nitrate], in the mills. There was a big board on the wall and you had to put down the time you put that powder in. And then you had to put the time when it had to come out. 'Cause if it was over that, it would blow the place to pieces.

Me and my friend had to work on the mills. Nobody else in there. We were shut in. It was like secret see and nobody else could go in. And if something went wrong, only us two was in there. It was very dangerous. But one of us would be watching

'I opened the door and half the house was gone'. Annie Slade at eight

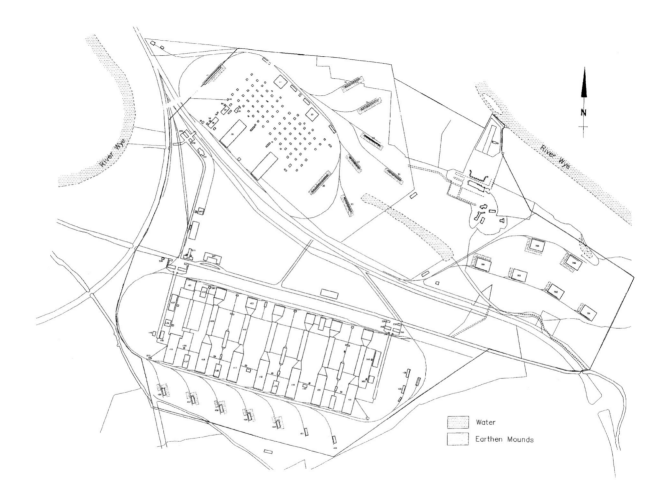

Extract from a map of the site made in 1919

the times with the mill and we use to 'ave five minutes sleep in this cart where the containers was. Then I'd go and watch the mills and she'd go in.

I'm only two weeks in there and then they'd send us to the stemming room where the shells was. You had to put the powder into the shells in the stemming room. But when we were on the mills, there was a little cart and there was some tins for you to put all the powder in. Containers. And they'd take that to the stemming room and let it go cold before you could put it in the shells. It 'ud be there for a couple of days.

It was very secret there. Me and my friend, we had to work nights for two weeks and then we'd go to the stemming room for two weeks and back again on the mill. At night we'd go to the canteen, and have a couple of bottles of milk. We got to drink a lot of milk because of the powder. Cause I had a mask — we had to wear masks on our face and only show your eyes to see what you were doing — and my hair was curly it used to poke out. It went all green in the front with the powder.

We used to put notes in the shells for the soldiers. On the top. I had a letter from an Australian fella. He was in the army.

When we were on nights we had two breaks to go to the canteen like. The food was not very good. Not much meat. When we used to got to the canteen at night all these Lancashire girls, they'd be step dancing on the tables! And we'd be playing the tin plates, you know? They used to wear clogs. They used to put them on to go into the canteen. They couldn't wear them in the factory. They used to leave them in the canteen, see, and then they'd change there.

'When the shells are dry, each one must be painted with two circles, which are known as "rings".' Jessie Sarah Derry from Ocle Pychard began work at the paint shop in Rotherwas in 1915. She kept a notebook about what she needed to do

I say it was dangerous work, but we had fun. We enjoyed ourselves.

A Zeppelin come over one night and the factory lights twinkled and went out. Some of the workers had their hands off with the machines. There was a few 'ad their fingers off. They were working on the machines and the lights gone out see: so the fingers … chop! When we seen the lights twinkling we had

to stop the machine, you know, with the powder in the mill. They had air raid shelters outside, but we had to stay where we were. Couldn't run, because if you run out you'd get caught in anything. Some of them tried to get out and of course they got injured and killed by trying to run out of the factory, see.

I was there about three years. I worked there till the peace was signed. We were all in lorries in our munition clothes going around Hereford with flags the day peace was signed.

I went into service then and then I got married. I went to service over Ferndale and I met my husband there. 'Cause he was in the First World War. He was in the trenches for four and

Kezia Clifford (front row, left) worked as a munitions worker in the First World War, seen here with other workers

The late Alfred Evans recalls Rotherwas during the First World War

My family was running the Wye Inn from 1912. In 1914 the war broke out and we were there during the war. Very strict my parents were, they didn't drink and didn't smoke: they should never have had that pub really. There was a hundred acres of wheat standing in August, some of the finest wheat in the country. They cleared all that and built the factory. It was in operation in a very short time and it employed thousands.

They put a bridge, attached to the river bridge, across the river for bicycles and people to walk from the town. This was down the bottom of Hampton Park Hill — the railway bridge is still there, but the overhang they put on for the people to cycle and walk is down. They put a path all the way along the river and fenced it in so that nobody could fall in the river.

We were very busy then, the Wye Hotel was. We came under the D.O.R.A., Defence of the Realm Act. 'We're under Dora', we used to say, and were only to open one hour in the midday.

Before they had any canteens there, when they were building the place, the tea boys used to come up and we used to fill all their bottles. They used to come at 11 o'clock and we filled hundreds of bottles and cans to take down to the navvies.

They would pay over the money and we would hand the beer over to them at 12 o'clock. We used to open the doors and they came in, the men, four deep. Four wide in through the double doors into the bar, the place was packed for one hour. We had to put doors on the staircase to stop them going into the bedrooms. You couldn't use the beer engines because of the froth. Instead we put it in galvanised baths, that you wash the clothes in, so we had two or three of those in there and one was pumping and filling them and another was dipping the mugs in and putting it out like that. It wasn't a glass mug, they were pink outside and white, clay I suppose it would be, earthenware.

We did have one hairy scare during the First World War. A Zeppelin, I think, got as far as Worcester and the girls came out of the factory by the hundreds. They were all in their overalls covered with TNT and picric acid, their hair and hands were yellow. I'd never seen them like this before. It was at night and they conveniently fainted outside the Wye, I suppose they had run half a mile or three-quarters. That was our excitement during the war.

a half years. And when he come home his father and mother said he was lousey. They had to take him down the shed, down the garden, strip him off. He had a beard and everything 'cause they couldn't shave. He said the Prince of Wales was in the trenches for a year with them.

His brother, he was in the war with him, but he went out one night to this battle on Hill Sixty and he never come back. He must 'ave been blown to pieces. They never knew. They never found out where . . .

Elizabeth Yemm of Hom Green, middle row, left, with her fellow First World War munitions workers in their overalls and mob caps

And then another brother was in the Second World War. He was in a Japanese camp and a couple of days before he was due to come home he drunk water. An' there was poison in it and he died. His mother was waiting for him to come home, bought a new bed, shaving stuff, everything and his friends in the camp with him come to visit the mother and brought his mug and things back with them. And they told her that he was dead. He was only 21.

Yes, the two of them went. Two brothers. One in the First World War and the other in the Second. I had five cousins altogether. One was blown down flying, another was killed on the beaches. That's the way. And they're looking for another war. Terrible 'en 'et?

I went back to Rotherwas the other day. I could have cried when I went by those gates. I know it was dangerous but we had good fun.

War was in the Air

When the Munitions Factory started to build up, my father went to work there in 1937. They sort of knew that there was bound to be a war. When Chamberlain came back with that piece of paper, it was stalling for 12 months while we built up.

In 1936 there was some clandestine reconstruction in the South Section of the factory. By 1937 the *Hereford Times* reported the transfer of the Woolwich factory to Hereford. Hereford would be one of five locations; the others were Chorley in Lancashire, Bridgend in Glamorgan, Pembroke Dock and Irvin in Ayrshire, with factories at Blackpole to the west of Worcester and Birtley in Durham. The programme would cost £25 million. In May 1937 Sir Thomas Inskip announced to the House of Commons: 'A filling factory at Hereford will be brought into full operation'.

Rotherwas was open from the First World War and kept going between the two wars, on a caretaker basis, run by the Royal Army Ordnance Corps. Later it became the Royal Ordnance factory. They started increasing the staff in 1936.

Some people thought we were rubbish, working there. These people didn't know what work was. Some thought: 'Fancy working there!' But if we hadn't it would have been a poor look out.

There were a terrific variety of people came there for jobs, including some people who hadn't worked in their life — amongst the better off, shall we say. Gradually they left again — before the days when you were not allowed to leave.

I was born in Hereford. My mum had my sister when I was two, then she died. Auntie Mary took to my sister, my

Customers outside the Vine Inn in Blueschool Street in the 1930s. Soon most of the young men will be in uniform

Melvin Angel (top right, back row) remembers a Bristol Blenheim fighter bomber having to land on the Lugg Meadows in 1939. 'Soldiers billeted at Lugwardine Court stood guard over the plane until it could be taken away on a transporter'

grandparents took to me, my dad kept my brother. I lived with my grandparents and then I went to the laundry, and then to Newport. I was in domestic service in Newport and they bombed Newport. That's what made me come home.

I came back and stopped with my auntie and started working at the factory. On my first day I was on day shift and I had to be up at the station for 5.30. It was terrible. I was just over 20. At first it was frightening 'cause you didn't know what was going to happen. You're a bit nervous, but eventually you got used to it. You just took chances didn't you?

We came to Hereford in 1930. There was a small munitions factory in Worcester, and through somebody father heard of this at Hereford. In March 1938 we moved to Rotherwas. You go on the road to Holme Lacy underneath the railway bridge, then you come to the main entrance, with the police all on the right hand side, and a big gate into the factory on the left hand side. Our property adjoined that.

I can remember running over to the police headquarters one night in my nightie because my mother was taken poorly, for they had a phone to reach the doctor. I remember the policeman who was on duty telling me: 'Now calm down. Tell us what?' I was all het up.

Behind us was Mr. Broaden, who was the chief accountant there. My father, Albert Griffiths, was a fitter by trade and residential fitter here. I don't really know what he did. I was 16. I went to work in a draper's shop, Davies in Eign Street. I was there five years and then I left and I went as cashier to Burtons the Tailors on the corner. I was there five years but left there when I got married.

There was war in the air, you know, and the factory was all getting primed ready for it. You could sense it, although dad never told us anything about the factory. You could sense that it was getting primed up. It must have been 1938.

The powder boys, as we used to call them, used to come with very big container vans and bring the powder down from Stockton on Tees. They would stay overnight to get it unloaded, and mother always put them up while they were there. They never seem to bother that they were carrying dangerous stuff.

They didn't put on women for a time. It was one of the rules that they did not employ women and then they had to be over 21. But later as the war progressed, they had to put on all women, who came from all round Herefordshire and into South Wales. They used to be brought in on buses mostly. Those from the Ross area came by train into the sidings at Rotherwas.

The local newspaper was carrying advertisements every week for people to be taken on at Rotherwas, and it was advertised as 'Royal Ordnance Factory'. Well my acquaintance with 'Ordnance' then was to do with maps! I didn't realise it had anything to do with munitions, not that that made any difference. They were busy putting on as many staff as they could get up, because they obviously knew what was coming. And they were busy re-arming.

I was working on the land and I had two kiddies. It was so wet I thought I can't go on the land. So they said they would have the kiddies for me so I started there.

We stayed at school until we were 14. And then I went to a farm. I never had no basic education at all, it was just earning a few shillings. I left the farm and then it came around, look, you had to do war work of some description. And of course munitions was applying for people to go to Hereford, so I went there.

They came from all over the country. My friend took one of the girls home with her as she found her crying one day because

'We would do all the men's work,' recalls Angela Francis from Sutton St. Nicholas with war-time friends Bubbles, Chris and Jean at their factory near Madley. In 1941 she watched as a member of Hitler's war cabinet, Rudolph Hess, was taken off an aeroplane at RAF Madley before being taken on to Abergavenny

she was so unhappy. She came from Scotland. My friend's mum looked after her. It was like a second home: she stayed there until she got married.

When war was declared I was in the Women's Services. I was called up on a Sunday afternoon and I cried all the way to barracks. We went to Norfolk and we used to drill on the front when there was ice and we'd all be falling down. It was very cold that winter. While we were waiting to go to the Middle East, to pass the time they sent us on a route march. That means you all go wherever they say you go, and we were trudging along, freezing cold, and the cocky little sergeant major came along, stopped and looked at us, and said: 'Blimey! What time's the funeral?'

I was on my knees brushing up some crumbs on the floor underneath the radio when it was announced.

I remember war being declared. I was working down at the farm that Sunday when war was declared. My brother-in-law died in the submarines and I was working there that day when the telegrams came to say. That's how my sister come to work at the munitions, because she was a war widow. She had a boy to bring up.

I knew I'd be called up, because I was already a Territorial. And we used to get the paper every day to see the war's a bit nearer, and now when we heard on the wireless that England had declared war, that was it. We all had to go and get ourselves together and go and do our job. It all seems very unreal now. It doesn't seem possible that it happened.

I think England would always cope, whatever time there's a war, I think she'll always cope. People are patriotic aren't they? They put their country first. If we haven't got a country, what have we got? Nothing! You've got to have a country haven't you?

Royal Ordnance Factory, Rotherwas

I can remember all the bikes coming up the road here, hundreds of bikes when the shifts changed over. Women on bikes, men on bikes. They'd be right across the road.

If you missed the bus you'd have to run from St. Martins church all the way down to Rotherwas. You'd have to go like the clappers to book on to your shift.

The factory was divided in two by the road from Hereford to Holme Lacy, known as the Straight Mile, possibly because it was used between the wars for street racing along a measured mile. On the left of the Straight Mile lay the North Section, on the right the South Section. Production started with 25 pounder shells and 3.7 inch anti-aircraft ammunition. Conditions at the factory were much the same as anywhere else, often dirty, often hard, but always dangerous.

When I first went there I did a spell filling shells and that sort of thing. In the Fillers, as we called it, we had North and South. The North did a lot of the sailors' stuff, depth charges and things for the navy. We filled mostly on the North.

You were a gang. There was so many for Fill, so many for the navy, where you put cordite on top of the navy shells. And depth charges were like our bins — they were all filled with powder and sealed and of course they went down in the water didn't they? We only did the filling there and it was transported away. Where it went to I don't know.

North Section

The North Section featured sheds with massive concrete blast walls that housed the Filling units where shells were filled. Roads were raised and floors covered with bituminous mastic to reduce the risk of sparks. Further up was the East Side. The buildings were all separate because of the possible accidents. We hadn't been there very long when there was an incident — we heard a bang but we didn't know, weren't told anything.

Sewing cordite bags, there used to be ten of us round this table. But it made you very sleepy, the cordite, and if someone was dropping off they would start singing to keep them awake. We were on what you would call the Clean Side: if you go down the Straight Mile you go to the left where Thorn Lighting was: that was the Clean Side. There were huts, not Nissen huts but made of concrete. You had the different shops like Shop 1, Shop 2. They did different things. On the right hand side was the Powder: go down the Mile on the right hand side where Opella is now — that used to be the Powder. I think it was TNT. It made them go yellow!

The filling factory, showing the two lines from which the shells were hung, two lines coming together where the shells were filled, then separating again

Well I never went over that side luckily. The left side was the Clean Side and the right side was the Dirty Side. As you went in you had take pins out or anything like that or anything silky — you practically had to strip off! They gave us these long coats to wear: white, they were, not like the cotton ones they wear today. These were horrible, buttoned right up to the neck. And they used to search you as you went in to see if you had any hairgrips or anything. These had to be left in the office where you were searched.

I was working with bundles of cordite. You got these like candles, about six or nine inches long. You had to tie them into bundles, put your foot through a stirrup, tie them up and when they're done put them in a box. We used to sit round a table. Most days everyone would choose a tune, go round the table and everyone would say a song and we'd all sing it. When it came to me it was always Nellie Dean.

I didn't like it there so I got married. My husband was a trucker on the Dirty Way. They had to wear special clothes to go on the Dirty Way, leave their own clothes in the room and put these Dirty Way clothes on.

The work was boring, it was tedious. The cordite was just like fine horse hair, beige. It was all weighed and cut to a certain length, and we just used to have the core which was about the size of your finger. When it come it was just like sheaths of corn to look at. When they cut it up it was only in short lengths and then you had a core and one that was smaller still and you had to wrap the outer one around it, tie it three times, two atop and one the bottom. You had to tie the charges a certain way, a certain knot otherwise it would fly all over the place and come undone. Once it touched the floor, it was rejected straight away; caused friction you see, so they were sweeping up all the time you see, it was kept beautiful.

Then the outside, you wrapped around the bigger one. Your foot was in a stirrup, so you could hold it. For a twelve hour shift, you had your foot in the stirrup, sat there on this hard stool and this long table, women either side, 12 one side and

12 opposite and another table the same. All the shops were spaced apart for safety sake. And the scissors that we used were brass, not to cause friction you see, or copper.

You didn't have any protection on your hands. You could talk, you could sing. There'd be seven or eight and a woman at the end with the big horse tails, as we used to call them, cutting them to size. Then you had the forewoman there watching all proceedings. She was all right. Somebody would start having a sing song and you'd all join in if you knew the words, if you didn't know the words you made them up.

I was on the North Section, tying and weighing cordite. It had to be a certain weight. They was already in lengths in a box. There was a special way of tying them, top and bottom. Then you pack them in another box and when they were full, the chap would come out and take them.

I was on the North side of the factory and I was an examiner checking the bombs. There's a certain measurement. You had a gauge. They had to be a certain depth, if not we rejected them. The factory workers were on piecework so, of course, they didn't like us too much if we sent any back.

South Section
On the Dirty Side they used to do just a bit of painting, things like that. I don't really know what they did, but they could wear anything they liked on the Dirty Side. Clean and Dirty meant explosives and non explosives.

There were about 20 where we were, but they were in three sections: there was the Fill where they used to fill these mines — it was stuff that would run like liquid. Then on up a bit they used to mix the powder — there was so much of one powder and so much of another that they used to mix. Then there was Transit where they used to go on the railway tracks to go away. A railway went along and that was where they used to put them on the trucks.

Number 1 was land mines. Little ones, the cake tins we used to call them. In Number 4, you had to have special shoes, special gowns, special hats because of the powder and by the time you'd finished there you were yellow. Number 5 was where they kept the gunpowder. It wasn't a healthy place to work in.

On the South side where the powders were, some of it was powder and some of it was like toffee. I couldn't have worked down there because of the smells and the taste went in your mouth and I used to faint easily. We were called out one day to go over to what they called Empty Shell. We had to put the empty shells into this container that held it while the paint was put on it. I think it was 25 pounders we were doing. After doing the 25 pounders you were moved on to the anti-aircraft, making fuses in the same way as the smaller ones. What a boring job. It wasn't hard work, it was boring, absolutely boring.

The South like, that was the main part where all the bombs were filled and everything. It was quite a big set up really. I forget how many of us was in the shop — we called them shops, you know.

People still say that the powers that be should have stood up to Hitler. But they hadn't got anything to stand up with!

We had fun. We used to sing you know, to keep us awake. I would start off the song, and then all would sing.

I was born in 1923. My husband went to the army in January 1939, when he was called up. I was 18. I was the youngest

in our shop and I was married. Our foreman, I used to tie her shoelaces together! I used to tie her shoes to the chair and she always knew! If anything happened to her, she always knew it was me that did it! I forget her name, but she was great she was! Putting things in your pocket, you know to make you jump. We would always play jokes on one another.

One chap who came to work, who lived in Bromyard, was Titch Corrigan, a very short man, little Titch. Before the public transport started running from Bromyard, he used to cycle in. But you could rely on Titch being there whatever the weather was. People who lived far nearer would not turn in, would make a claim for what they called 'stress of weather'.

One of his jobs was carrying huge buckets of TNT, and he was so short that, of course, they

dragged on the ground! But he delighted in new people who came to work there, and used to play tricks on them.

If you were working in the Powders as they called it, which was the TNT, you were entitled to a dose of carbonated mixture, which was to counteract the stomach pains which could be caused by inhaling TNT. His favourite trick with new people was taking them to the central stores where huge jars of carbonated mixture were kept, and dosing them with it. It was a laxative, a cleanser, so to speak. They wouldn't make the toilet half the time! That used to amuse little Titch! Well, he was getting his own back for tricks that were played on him.

Mr. Broaden got in touch with mum or, most likely, dad and asked if I would go and work in the factory, in the offices there, because they knew I'd done some office work. Of course dad said: 'She's not here; she's in London'. But he said: 'Sis is here'. Mr. Broaden knew both of us girls and they offered Sis the job. My sister was in the transport office. She used to issue the travel vouchers because any that lived out in the country, they had to have travel vouchers.

You had to mix, I'm not being a snob, but you had to mix with who you were put with. And there was some characters there, I can tell you. We were very shocked. Oh, I made some nice friends there. Quite a lot of nice friends and people older than myself. Young, well married women that came in part-time.

I'll tell you something, it finished my education off. I was a country lass when I went there. I hadn't been there very long before I was well educated.

During the war I was working in West Street at W.R. Jones and Son. I was Manageress there then, because Clive Jones's son had joined the R.A.F. Mr. and Mrs. Jones senior were too old to do very much work. As the men were all called up, I got deferred from going in the forces. I wanted to go in the forces. I wanted some excitement. A lot of people used to say you wouldn't like it. I don't know. But I liked it in the Girls Training Corps. We did wear uniforms and do things.

Men at the factory were few and far between.

I was the Chief Worktaker. When my wife was told I'd been made Chief Worktaker, somebody had told her I'd become chief undertaker! Eventually I had 100 Worktakers, which included six Senior Worktakers. You had the three grades. Worktaker, Senior Worktaker, and one Chief Worktaker. The latest figures I have seen was 2,000 workers, but I was under the impression there were a lot more than that, because my staff was based on one Worktaker for every hundred workers.

We took particulars of the work that people were doing, such as cleaning shells and bombs, then filling them, and then fusing them, and then loading them away in railway trucks, to go to various destinations.

There used to be an old boy in Ross who worked in what they call the Fuses. He was the Trucker. And he'd always say: 'Ay bugger 'em'. Very often when we used to meet him in Ross afterwards I'd think to myself: 'Here comes Mr. Buggerem'.

I started work at 14 simply because a lot of the teachers were in the T.A. in those days and were called up, reducing schooling to four hours a day, sometimes three hours a day.

I was an apprentice electrician and we were doing contract work in there as an apprentice. It was such a huge place. Ninety percent of them were women and if you went through the sheds to get where we were working there would be all these women on benches with all the shells. You got all cat calls just like men do to women. And the women were worse actually. Of course being about 15 I was rather embarrassed at that age and rather naive. I'm glad I wasn't working amongst them, that's all I can say.

What did you do in the War, Mummy?

Three processes are involved in the making of armaments: the engineering factory where the shell cases, guns and hardware are made; the explosives factory where explosives are made; and finally the filling factory where the two processes are brought together.

In 1939 there were engineering factories at Birtley, Co. Durham, Dalmuir at Clydebank, Blackburn in Lancashire and in Nottingham. There were explosives factories at Waltham Abbey and Irvine in Ayrshire. ROF Rotherwas was one of the major filling factories in the country. Of the three kinds of armament factories, it was also the most dangerous.

What an awful thing, war. Making bombs to kill other people.

I was one of the first 50 women who joined at the beginning and I was there right the way through. In 1944 when the explosion happened, I was there. It was men: it wasn't girls, girls wasn't in that, on the big stuff. They used to do land mines in bombs. Oh they used to be massive, I mean they used to be strung up in the air. But as I said the men used to work on that.

I started off putting lutin round fuses. It was like putty really, it was a sealer and you put it round the edge of the fuse, before it goes on the shell. I started on that, but I wasn't on that for long. Then I went on the presses. You put six shells on a trolley, and it used to go in a cubicle where the press made a hole in each middle. You closed the door and worked the press by levers and mirrors. The hole was made for the fuse.

And then they altered everything. They altered the conveyor belt that come right from the bottom of the unit right up to the top. And shells used to come up very, very, very slow for the

A formal picture of Munitions Workers. Sent by Sandra Watson from Australia whose mother Clohilda May Dickinson cycled daily from the Forest of Dean to work at the factory

TNT, 'cause it was boiling hot when it was put in the shells. The men used to do that. The shells came in trays of four. And people on the conveyor belt, they used to do little different jobs. I used to fuse them. That was to get more production.

There was another girl; we used to work each side of the table. And when sat we were in with the other girls they would put great big, what they called glass balls around us. We were sealed off from everybody. You couldn't see nobody.

To put in the fuse you had to take it out of this tray — they were in steel cups. You had to take it out, put it in a vice, tighten your vice up and then you had a key. You had to give it one good jerk to make sure you got it down right.

Then you had to loosen it out of the vice, and pick it up and put it on the table. You were only allowed so many fused shells on the table at once. I don't remember whether it was 20 or 25. Yes, and we used to have a man with a hand wheeling truck, like, and he used to have to put them on the truck and take them down into transit. Happy soul: we used to call him Smiler.

My job when I started there was on night shift — when we went down for interview in the morning, the local people were sent home again to return for the night shift. For the first fortnight there was a frost every night, and handling shells which were coming in covered with frost was not very pleasant. A lot of the equipment was not too good at the beginning.

With the shell you had a cardboard tube that went down in when you're filling. When it reached a certain stage, you'd hold the tube upright and fill in around it with what they called Amatol, which was a mixture of TNT and ammonium nitrate, if it was a bomb, or pure TNT if it was shells. The cardboard tubes were put in so as to leave a space for the exploder and the fuse: the exploder actually went down in the tube and the fuses were screwed in the top after.

Women's work was never done. Many women like Eve Lichfield joined the Herefordshire Land Army Girls

To start I was in this Number 2. That was where they had 25 pounders. I had to clean the top screw that goes into the shell, because in that screw there was always some powder that got stuck in there. We had to clean that out before they put the stopper on or else it would have gone off before time.

Then they wanted volunteers to go work in Number 7 so me and four other girls volunteered and it was much nicer. We were on the Clean Side, that was the mines and depth charges. We didn't have any shells, not where we worked, but we used to do

Like many other First World War munitions workers Jessie Derry had a studio portrait taken of herself in her munitions clothes

Nora Foster (née Davies) remembers her days as a radio announcer at the factory

I went in 1940 when I was 20. When I first went down I had an office job and I worked there for a couple of years. Then they appointed an entertainment manager and he decided he'd do something about getting entertainment for the workers and he approached me. I don't know why. I rather think he liked blondes and I was blonde then. He was rather fond of the ladies. He said, would I like to work with him on entertainments? We would have our little broadcasting studio, we could choose and play records for the workers during their meal break, and we met the people who came to entertain.

There were three of us and we were on shifts and it was our job to meet these entertainers and make sure they had something to eat in the meal break and introduce them to the workers.

We were working on our own in a little studio which was maintained by a man who had an electric shop in Hereford. He went on to keep the Grey Friars restaurant, his name was Edmond Campion. We had a speaker and quite a sophisticated machine. I didn't know much about it, but we knew where to speak — there was a volume control with a needle and we knew if we were speaking too loud. If the meal break coincided with something from the BBC then we just switched it over to that.

They had loudspeakers in the various units they were working in so it could come across to them. It was like music while you work to encourage them. They could ask for requests in their meal break, so we'd have a whole lot of requests to play. If we weren't playing requests we could have a whole pile of records on the spindle and play them. We were allowed to choose new records every couple of months to enlarge our record library.

'Clair de lune' — I loved that one. I remember Bing Crosby's 'You Are My Sunshine' was one of the workers' favourites: I hated playing that. It almost wore the ridges out, it was played that often.

Some people were sending requests and we played them in all innocence. Some were played as a joke: one that was requested, 'My Curly Haired Baby', was for someone expecting a baby when she shouldn't have been! When that was realised the requests had to go through a shop steward, and if he thought they were alright then we played them.

When they went for their meal break we had these entertainers, people from E.N.S.A. Anna Neagle, the film star, came. She was playing somewhere in Hereford and they persuaded her to come. We met them and introduced them to the workers and made sure they had refreshments.

There was Billy Milton, he wasn't terribly well known, but he came and sang, and Elton Hayes, he was a balladier in a film about Robin Hood. There was an R.A.F. station at Credenhill and one at Madley and the concert parties would come from these places to entertain. Sometimes they would have local people. One fellow, he used go round the meadows singing in a high voice. It was considered very odd for a man to sing like that, but he enjoyed singing and they would ask him to come and sing and they would bang on the tables with their spoons. He thought he was the bees knees, but they were really taking the mickey. He used to sing 'It's a Sin To Tell a Lie'.

Nora Davies, one of the radio broadcasters at ROF Rotherwas. 'Vera Lynn was on an awful lot at that time' recalls munitions worker Molly Meyrick

small mines, the ones they put along the beaches. We used to have great big ones about 12 foot long, but there was no explosives in them. They were waiting to be filled and detonated whenever.

I worked in Unit Two. That's where the 25 pounders were made. And then I went into Unit One. At one time I didn't have any periods, so therefore I was in Empty Shells for a while because they thought the powder was affecting

me. And then I used to make U.P.s as they called them, trench mortars.

I often had a bit of stick to push the powder thing down because it was very hard to keep doing it with your thumbs. You weren't allowed to use sticks. The only thing you could get it down with was your two thumbs and if you were caught using a stick to do it, God it could have gone off you see. We used to find anything we could do it with and hid it. It was nearly as bad when we did the trench mortars in Unit One.

We had to have a pass to show at Ross station, and when we got off we used to walk up and have a cup of tea at the canteen. There used to be two policemen

ready to search you, quite natural. Then we walked up and were shown to our destinations and what we had to do. We had to be trained in what to do and how to handle the goods.

We used to sort the fuses out, then go into the Fill and sort out the clean fuses. Then the C.I.A.s would check on every shell that came through. There would be a couple of foremen and a long table. They used to watch us. Could be 10-20 at a table. We had to make sure they were alright before they went into the filling and put on. The men used to bring the empty shells and they would take them through to a certain place. It was nerve-racking to a certain extent, because you didn't know whether

May Morgan, second from the right, with other workers at the munitions factory in the last World War

29

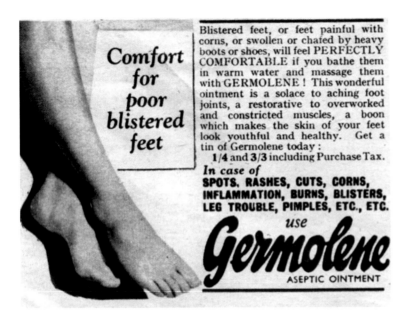
the fuses would go off. You would do the fuses in a cubicle for a couple of days and then go into the main building where the shells came through, checking them to see if they were clean. And then they went on down. One of the men would pick them up, put them in a trolley. Where they went to after that we don't know.

If you stopped to think of what you were doing, I don't think you could do it. Well, you didn't.

Civil Inspection of Armaments

C.I.A. that's what we were called. There used to be an overseer over us. I can see her now. She used to always wear something red on her hat. It was to show who she was.

When I was 18 I opted to work at Rotherwas. I joined the Civil Inspection of Armaments. Pay packets fluctuated because of the number of hours worked, night shifts being the most profitable. We wore different clothes: the workers wore khaki or navy overalls and their hair was tied up into a scarf affair whereas the C.I.A.s wore white overalls, white beret and sported a red armband with C.I.A. in white.

Our supervisors wore red berets and were known to us as Red Caps. Hair grips, slides, suspenders and jewellery were banned.

Rotherwas was under contract to Woolwich arsenal and the C.I.A. were employed by Woolwich to examine and pass all stages. Each inspector had their own personal stamp so that any accidents could be traced back.

During my time the C.I.A.s were invited to volunteer to work away for a month. My most enjoyable outstation was when we checked goods at Aston Villa Football Club. Tin boxes were stored in rooms adjacent to the players' rooms at the back of the grandstand. We assembled, greased and reassembled and repacked the contents. We were told not to divulge our reason for being there.

C.I.A. were in charge. They used to check everything, to see if everything was in order before they left the floor. You had a foreman as well, two or three, or a forewomen.

Sometimes you'd be in a cubicle and you'd have to sort the fuses all out. Then they were taken into the main building. The cubicles were all in groups of four. You were watched all the time. You could talk to one another, it wasn't that bad. You'd go mad if you didn't. You could have a laugh and joke, but there was no hanky panky there. You couldn't even wear a slide or a brooch or a wedding ring. Majority of people left it at home, 'cause it wouldn't have been safe. Somebody would've pinched it.

We had a lot of men come from London — examiners. You had a chap that examined it to see that it was all clean and filled properly. A lot of them settled this way, you know? They didn't go back to the town.

We didn't do the filling of the shells. Sometimes you were yellow, your face went yellow. You had a hat and clothing to protect your hair and body.

They gave us something like a cake tin with a block of stuff in and you had to melt that stuff down and then put this other stuff in and you had to stir it. I said it's worse than making a cake this is. Somebody came behind me and said: 'You're not doing that right'. I turned round and it was my brother! He was a C.I.A. down there — I could have killed him.

Munitions work was hard and dangerous.
Many, like Margaret Duddington, Audrey Finney, Jean McGaw and Irene Hewitt, preferred the outdoor life of the Land Army

It did worry you though. We made these little cake things and you'd put the top on them and they'd go on to get the fuses in. Then they'd go on to the trolleys to go Dinedor Hill. We had no end stored up in there.

I was on Empty Shells as we called it, the filling place, cleaning the bombs, the shells. We did those very big ones, the length of a settee. They were the 200 pound ones I think. Mostly the men that weren't called up, they filled the bigger ones, but it

was a lot of hand filling, you know. I filled no end of shells and that down there. We wore gloves, a brown overall. We had to tie our hair up.

We had depth charges and the powder nearly killed you. It got on your chest and we all went ginger! Oh it was a dreadful place to turn your colour.

I moved on to filling bombs and shells. We had these conveyor belts. They came down. You would do one job, the person next

Now part of the Rotherwas Industrial Estate,
many former munitions buildings still survive

The COAL, GAS and ELECTRICITY you save help to build Merchant Ships

NOTE: A gas fire or electric oven uses 5 lbs. of coal in 2 hours

We must SAVE FUEL for Battle!

ISSUED BY THE MINISTRY OF FUEL AND POWER

to you would do another job — that's the way it went until you got to the end. You each had your little job to do.

I dropped one bomb on my foot one day and my big toe hasn't been right since. That's what the cordite bags were for. There used to be a cordite bag put in and then a little round thing, a shellack I think they called it, that was done to make up the explosives.

A munitions worker waits for her bus home at Redhill. Women moved from all over the country to work at the Munitions Factory

They'd come and pick so many from each line and then we'd do the tall ones and you'd put the screws in the bottom then they'd go down the line for something else to be done. That wasn't so bad.

We did a lot for the navy. They had big long shells and in the boxes we used to write notes and put in the boxes. They were going off to the boys. We used to write: 'Good luck, lads'. 'We are doing our share'. 'You keep going'. I don't know how many had them but we used to do it for devilment. Well, we did it for them so they knew we were thinking of them. We used to get the soldiers come round the factory: they used to ask us what we were doing.

My late cousin, Marjorie, was persuaded to put her name and address into a shell case and received a reply from a 19-year-old soldier. Being in her late 20s, she passed this address to me. I corresponded with this soldier for several months, but after D Day heard nothing so have presumed he lost his life.

What We Wore

There was the first gate under the bridge. The other side of the bridge we had to wear shoes like the prisoners — they had broad arrows. When we started our overalls also had broad arrows all over. The men used to say it was like being in prison, but everything you had was marked with broad arrows because it belonged to the government. After a while we did get plain overalls, but we still had broad arrows on our shoes. They were thick soled and hard. You had a job to bend your foot, you just had to walk flat. They were leather stitched. There was no metal buckle on them.

One day I had to go home in the factory shoes because somebody had pinched mine. Daps type of thing, soft, like little bootees with rubber soles. And you had a little hat or scarf to tie over your hair. You'd have to watch whether somebody would pinch your clothes. Coats or things like that. £10 for a pair of shoes in those days, it was a lot of money! There was a big changing room. Your uniform belonged to the factory. We had to take it off before we went home and hang it up. The ones who came on the next shift would probably borrow it.

First of all we had to clock on. We was searched. You took your own food and that was all left in the canteen. Then you went over the barrier and you were given a clocking card and number and that was put on your clothes. That number was on your kit bag so you put your outdoor clothes in there while you put on their clothes — which was your overall, cap and shoes. With arrows on everywhere.

You wasn't allowed to wear rings with stones in, hair grips or pins or anything that would cause friction. You could wear pure silk underwear but you couldn't wear artificial silk, you gotta wear cotton, everything was cotton. I'd get mine from Miss Colwell, a little shop at the top of Ross. It was lovely and I always had my stockings from there, pure silk stockings, pure

Kezia Clifford (front row, third from left) with other First World War munitions workers in their uniforms

silk brassieres, about size 33 — I was only little you see.

You paid for that out of your own money. Well Peacocks was there then, they used to sell cotton underwear, you had to give your coupons up for everything. My sister had children you see, so I used to give her money for the coupons.

They had a laundry at the factory and a doctor and nurse, indoor surgery and outdoor surgery. When time went on, they opened up more shops as we were doing the two shifts, 12 hours about a fortnight about. Then they turned it into three shifts — red, white and blue — three eight-hour shifts. You worked eight hours, but had one hour travel either way.

When I started first I had a white pair of trousers. Like a fluffy stuff, they were hot in the summer. And a jacket. They were men's. They didn't have enough overalls to go around and they gave us a pair of brown shoes and they had an arrow on the toe. If you tried to take it off, you could see where the holes were, where it had been stitched in. Of course you had to wear wellingtons as well in some of the jobs. A little round hat with all your hair pushed in, no rings, no jewellery, nothing; no pins in your hair, no pins in your clothes.

On the factory floor we had to wear these long white overalls coming down to our ankles. We didn't have belts and they were like nightgowns on us. They'd only just started having women on the South Section so it was a novelty. The men used to stand and whistle as we went by. Eventually they did issue us with a belt so it didn't look as bad. You had to wear something on your head. When I was Worktaker we could wear our own clothes because we just walked through the filling sheds, but we had to wear something on our head. I used to wear a beret. I was platinum blonde then but the hair that wasn't covered became a different colour by just walking through the sheds!

What We Earned

The wartime wages were a good incentive for going to work at ROF Rotherwas.

It was either the forces or the munitions for girls. I didn't want either. I had led a very sheltered life and I didn't want to go away from home so I had to go down there.

I was working in a farm at 14. Then it was decided I should go to the munitions so I went to the labour exchange and went to the munitions works straight away. I was earning 5 shillings a week on the farm and when I went to the munitions factory it was about £3 something.

In them days that sort of money was money you'd never seen before. I used to work in a house with a cook and a house maid, domestic work. We used to have 5 shillings a week to work in, so when I had wages of £3 to £4, and a bit more at holidays, I thought I was rich.

On the whole I settled in quite well there. I mean the money was very interesting, I didn't like the three shifts, but the two long ones were killing people — they were too long to work.

When we were two shifts and worked right through the night, the nights were very long. I never did care for the night shifts, but they were shorter in the end.

I was earning about 7 pence an hour on the land. When I started at the factory it was £1 18 shillings a week. Then £3 something. Every now and again it went up, didn't it?

We had more money then. We'd been a bit poor before, and their wages they considered very good. I got a friend, Betty, and she was doing wages in the office. And she said they had to take these wages out, with somebody with them, to the different huts.

Part of the Worktaker's job was calculating the incentive bonus which they were on, and the wages. We supplied them with the information as to the number of hours worked, wage per person, and what particular job they were on according to the different rates of pay. When they first started putting on extra people before the war the basic rate of pay was 29 shillings a week, plus an incentive bonus payment of £1 which for Herefordshire, which had low rates of pay anyway, was relatively high. Getting the money to above £3 was everybody's ambition.

I was earning five shillings a week on the farm and it shot up to three pounds something at the factory. Course I was working a damn sight harder. My mother worked hard as well — she used to take in laundry to make a few bob. I won't say she liked money but she liked having money behind her. But mind, those days were hard.

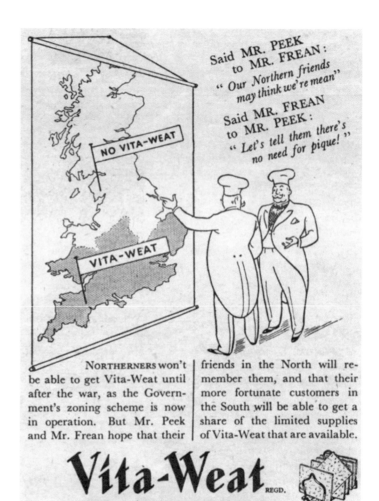

Shift Work

I worked a fortnight days and a fortnight nights when I was there. But then they changed it to three shifts.

When I started it was just days really 'cause they hadn't got enough girls to put two shifts on. Then they changed it like.

There were two shifts, 7.30 'till 6.30, night and day, the two different shifts.

When we were doing 12 hours we had three breaks: one in the morning; an hour for our dinner; then quarter of an hour in the afternoon. We used to have to go to the Empty Shell Store to drink our tea. We couldn't drink it in the Filling part.

We used to work three shifts. 7 till 2, 2 till 8 and then all night till 7 o'clock. I used to get the bus at Ryeford, where I lived, at 5.25 in the morning. We used to get home at 4 o'clock in the afternoon. We used to go at 1.30 in the afternoon shift and then we used to get home at something after 11 at night. Then on night shift we went at just after 7 o'clock I think it was, and we came home at something after 8 the next morning. One week after another, three weeks I'd go.

We all had soldiers as boyfriends, I'm not the only one. If we worked 2 p.m. 'till 10 p.m., all our boyfriends used to meet us from the train at 10 o'clock at night. Then they would be there the next night. I had one called Ken and a couple in the Royal Norfolks. Ken was in the Airborne. He was a friend of mine and still is now. The one I was going with in the Norfolks, he went out and was killed. He wasn't the only one. A lot went from here and they were stationed in Ross. Just one of those things. He got into Jap hands and that was it. I knew he was missing because all of my letters was coming back.

We did three shifts. Early mornings, afternoons and night shift. That was the way it followed: mornings first, afternoons and nightshift. I quite enjoyed the nightshift really.

You had a break to have your meal. It used to be lovely to go out and see the moon. Every window was blacked out. At home you know, everywhere and that was it. You dare not shine a light, no lights at all. It was completely black. You'd think twice about going anywhere, you know, in the dark.

Munition shortages

Do you remember being there? It was a Bank Holiday and we were supposed to have some time off. Somewhere was bombed — I don't know whether it was Coventry or what — during the night. They said they hadn't got enough shells to fire back and they asked everybody to work on so we stayed on instead of going home you know, we did the extra time. A double shift.

I understand that when the Battle of Britain was on, Rotherwas was the only factory supplying 3.7 anti-aircraft shells, and yet you still hear from time to time people saying 'we should have stood up to Hitler'. We'd got precious little to stand up with! That was the trouble.

The best part was getting your bath in the evening. You didn't get it in the day, only at night. There used to be about 20 baths, 10 down each side. It used to be lovely. Separate cubicles and you used to pull a curtain. For ladies only: no men. They had their own room. You'd get one about 3 a.m. You'd sit there, lay back and think: 'Oh I've only got half an hour and then get out'. We didn't have to take no towels. They supplied those because the laundry would do the washing. Then you'd have to go back to work because you worked from 10 p.m. 'till 6 a.m. You'd clock in at 10 o'clock then down the corridor to wherever you worked. It used to be four for me and sometimes you were put in a cubicle about six of you. Then perhaps the next night you'd be in the Fillings place. At about 3 o'clock the charge hand would tell you to take your bath and then when you came back someone else would be sent. That's how we done it. Then we'd clock off at 6, then go to the train, which would be waiting to take us back home.

They used to come round every so often, about two or three times a week, making you have a bath. I used to say I can have one at home. 'No, you're down for a bath. Here. You've got to have one'. We had to go and have a bath and the towels used to be brown. They couldn't help it; it was the colour in them, they turned the towels brown. I once ran the water and I didn't get in the bath; I just wet my feet because it used to leave a brown mark round the bath. You couldn't help it. It's a thing that wouldn't come off; you couldn't blame the one before you.

I used to go home and have a bath, but you'd still be the same when you came out, just a bit fresher. If anyone saw your clothes they knew you'd work at Rotherwas. The kids used to say: 'They work at Rotherwas!'

On nights, we were allowed to have half an hour for a bath. I think more or less it was to keep us awake. There used to be a long cubicle with several baths in there.

The Canteen

There were two canteens at that time in the early days. There was what they called the West Main canteen, that was near the first gate that you came to on the Straight Mile. And the second canteen was on the Straight Mile, but halfway up. When the canteens opened all they sold in the way of drink was cider.

The first night I was down there I had to go onto night shift and you had to take your own food and that disappeared during the

*One of the canteens during
the First World War*

night. It was eaten by rats. There were plenty of rats around, and the place was alive with rabbits.

The canteen was a big one on the main road. We used to have to change our shoes to go. They did cooked meals. You used to have to pay: you could have a dinner and a pudding. A cup of tea was a penny, then the main meal was about one and ninepence, but I used to wait 'till I got home to have my cooked meal.

There were four canteens down there. I was assistant manageress in the West Main most of my time. And then there was the north, south and east canteens. Four canteens. There were four of us as assistant manageresses. On nights we had a man who came with a van and took us round to collect the money from these canteens. And then I'd come back and put it away in the safe in the office in the West Main.

It was very nice, one time, because we had E.N.S.A. come round for entertaining. And Gracie Fields was there. We went across over to the Empty Shell place and we were entertained by Gracie Fields. It was lovely.

In the canteen it was sort of cheese and buns and bread and butter, and all sorts of things like that. Out of the canteen, there was a huge kitchen, where they would have cooked meals. In the canteen where I was, in the West Main, we had

At the start of the Second World War, Hereford Town Hall became the Food Office. Connie Williams worked there:

'The day war broke out — oh, what a beautiful day it was, that first Sunday in September 1939. But my husband was in the Hereford Territorial Camp at Weston Super Mare and therefore in the army from then on. It was a great shock to me as I had believed that peace was with us to stay. How was I going to manage on, what was it, one shilling a day? I went to the Labour Exchange and got an interview for a post at the Food Office and started there on the first Monday in October. We used the Town Hall's Main Hall — it made a big change from dancing in there! There was no overtime pay in those first few months and I often had to work late as the Town Clerk was also Fuel Officer, Billeting Officer, etc. But I didn't mind as I thought I was doing my bit for my country to help win the war.'

casks of beer and cider as well. You see, cheese, bread, beer, cider.

When you left your shift, just a bit further up the road there was a place where you could be called in to be searched. One of our women got caught with some butter on her. That was the end of her there. I was called in once, but of course I hadn't got anything on me.

I cycled to and from Dinedor, because I lived up on top of Dinedor hill which looked over the whole factory. When you got there and you had to clock in and then you get in the tea — tea urns ready, and the cups and saucers put out in place.

I can see the kitchens now, all the pans of rice pudding! Rice soaking on the top, on the hotplates. If the cook wanted anything out of the fridge, I would have to issue what she wanted. We were there all night. We're there with everything ready, so that when they come into the canteen we serve them with whatever they want. They had to pay for their meals. Each night I've got to cash up.

The people that had started it up, the canteen business, they were local Herefordians and then after a bit, it was taken over by Hancocks of Cardiff — Hancocks Brewery. Then I think, by the time I finished, it was called the Ministry of Supply.

The funniest thing I remember was we had this man to tap the beer and the cider barrels ready for us. Well I got on that night, and oh dear! The beer barrel hadn't been tapped. I thought I could do it, so I got hold of the tap, and the mallet, and I hit it in. But I didn't hit it strong enough and the beer

was shooting out! Some of the men that had come to be served, they jumped over the counter! We were mopping up the beer afterwards! Some got wasted. A man would hit it a lot harder I suppose.

We used to take our own sandwiches. By the time you'd queued up you didn't have time to eat what you'd ordered. Never used to eat hardly anything anyway, couldn't stand it. It was the taste in your mouth from the cordite. Working in the cordite for so long didn't affect some, but did me. No matter how many times you cleaned your teeth, you could still taste it.

In the canteen we could buy a cup of tea but we would take our sandwiches with us and we used to leave them in the canteen. We used to have a little old man, he was lovely. He couldn't sing, but fair play he used to sing 'Welcome Home'.

We didn't all go in together, we had to take it in turns, so that someone was always working all of the time. Two or three would go at one time and then some more at another time. That's how we worked. Then you could buy a cup of tea, normally to go home. The wages wasn't that high. If you earned £3 in those days it was a lot of money. When we got out of the canteen there used to be two huts and that's where you had to show your passes then you'd get further up, a little walk towards the gates, and there'd be two policemen there. Well they didn't always search you, but every now and again they'd pick on you and take you in to be searched and then you'd walk on up to the changing rooms.

There was men's special clothes same as what there were for the women. They had to wear protective clothes because of the powders. The men had brown suits.

You know we were such a crowd. When you went for a meal, oh the crowd was dreadful if you wanted to queue at the canteen. There were hundreds of us queuing for a drink. I used to take what mum had got with me, you know? I even took a teapot and a quarter of tea and begged a drop of hot water from the kitchen!

The canteen was away from the Fill. There was a special place they built for facilities. And we had the old bands playing you know, the older type of bands. Lovely music not like they got today. You had to write in and then they would say this or that has been requested. There was an awful lot of recording done that they played on the radio for us.

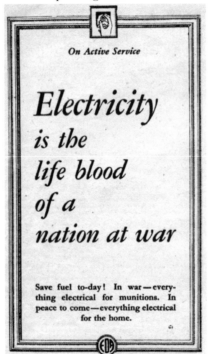

On Active Service

Electricity
is the
life blood
of a
nation at war

Save fuel to-day! In war—everything electrical for munitions. In peace to come—everything electrical for the home.

I was up around Farnborough, Clapton, Essex and I used to follow my husband around from one camp to another. I was a cook in the NAAFI in 1941. It wasn't what you'd call exciting. I didn't get on very well with the manageress because she was too dominant, and I was a bit wilful. She said to me one day I had to cook some meat, and it had been hanging around a lot. It didn't smell right to me, so I refused to cook it. And another time I got into trouble because I was using the tea cloth to open the ovens, and she told me off about that. Oh, and I was singing in the NAAFI, and I got in trouble for that as well, so I said 'right' and I walked out. They couldn't stop me because I'd volunteered to do the job.

I was manageress for a short while and one of the girls was selling Guinness and underpricing. Instead of one and six, she sold it for ninepence, so therefore I was hundreds of pounds down. I had to make that up somehow, so I told the cook, and she said: 'That's alright. We'll make some meat pies'. So we made some extra pies.

Of course, when I left, they wrote and asked could I please explain how I made £400 profit while I was there! Because she went on making the pies, you see, and I forgot to stop her! The NAAFI don't like that. They think you're fiddling.

Keep It Secret

They used to have a railway through to take all the bombs and that away, but where they went to we didn't know.

Explosives can be dangerous if they're mishandled and from time to time there were minor explosions which were not talked about. The newspapers weren't allowed to carry any stories, which they probably could have done.

Men worked with the powder more so than what the girls did. It wouldn't have been safe for us to be filling shells. One man used to bring a dozen from, I should think, Shell 2 or could have been 1, up the corridor. Then he used to come through and take them through to another department, but what went on in there we don't know. Whether they went into store, which could of happened, we don't know, because if you went up the corridor there was always someone watching you. Quite understandable because you don't know who was about.

He was very quiet. He would never tell you about the work that was going on. I used to tap him once or twice, but he would never say anything. If they were all like him the enemy wouldn't have got much information!

It was all hush hush really. You weren't supposed to talk about it. You were warned gossip was dangerous. It was a very peaceful place actually. A lot of different people worked there but they was so afraid of sabotage that, I think, you were told to curb your tongue. You couldn't say 'I filled 20 or 30 shells today'. You weren't supposed to talk like that.

They were very secretive, you see. The local papers and the national newspapers were not allowed to publish things during the war.

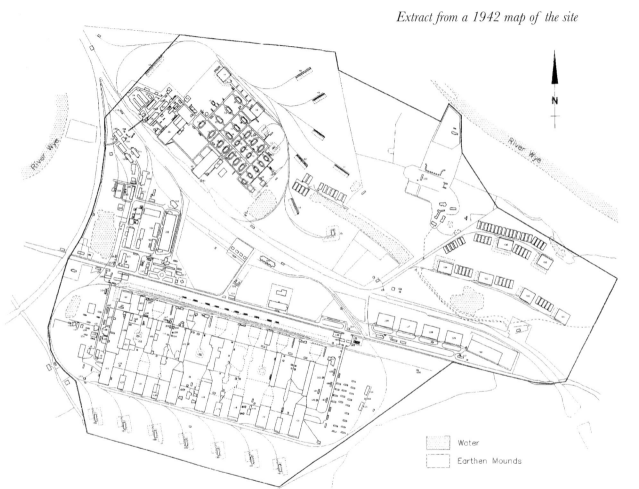

Extract from a 1942 map of the site

Rules & Discipline

There were two rulebooks published. One thing that we were laughing about — no running! You weren't allowed to run. There was no need to tell people to do that when they were going to work, but as soon as it was knocking off time, you'd hear the cry go out 'stop running!'

They had time clocks. Redhill Brookes, I remember, was the name of the makers of the clocks. They clocked one another's cards if they weren't detected.

They had what they called Danger Books. You had to hand them all in when you left.

There was a search room when you went through the last gate. The police would just pick someone out and search them. You weren't allowed to have cigarettes or sweets in your pocket. If you had anything it was taken back to the place where we had to leave our coats.

You weren't allowed to wear necklaces or rings. But the ones who worked in the Empty Shed could wear anything they liked. We weren't allowed to have a zip or metal buttons. Anything that was metal could set off a spark: no grips in your hair — you had to put this turban on and push all your hair into it. You weren't supposed to have any hair showing.

We used to have a chap as worked for Charlesworth Bodies in Gloucester. He used to bring up pigs and cut them up on the benches until somebody reported him. He was killing pigs and used to bring the pork up there and cut it up and sell it, which was against the law! You couldn't have took anything into Rotherwas munitions like that.

Men used to get snuff in there. That was against the law mind. You could always tell if they'd got snuff because their handkerchiefs would be yellow, not only with the powder, but with the ruddy snuff as well. And you'd very often see 'em get in the corner saying: 'Do you want a bit?'

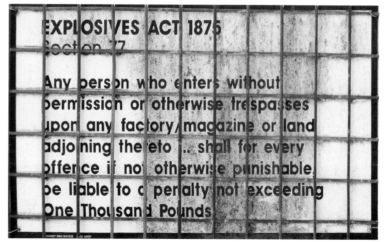

You couldn't just walk in, you had a pass. You had to get off your bike, show your pass and walk through, you weren't allowed to ride through. If it was your boyfriend or something, usually they'd take you as far as the gate, and then they would have to leave you. You didn't ask them in normally.

One worker wondered why she and her friend were pulled out for security checks on numerous occasions by a particular policewoman. She thought nothing of it until an older female worker told her the policewoman fancied her and her friend. 'How can she fancy me? I'm a woman', she said.

I was given an office over in the second block. The central office staff were not allowed into the danger areas, 'cause you had to produce your pass to go in. And also, when you went in, you were asked: 'Have you any prohibited articles?' which chiefly meant tobacco, cigarettes and matches. Usually you didn't wait for the War Department police to ask, you just said: 'No prohibited articles'. In the early days when one or two people got pulled in for having cigarettes or matches with them, they were also prosecuted. Later, when they were glad of more people to work there, they dropped that. One, who was found in the Wye Pub when he should have been on duty, was hauled up before the Principal Clerk.

You couldn't go on the Clean with dirty shoes. You had to be careful there were no bits on the bottom of your shoes. They were pretty desperate over that. The police girls used to come round the shops — we used to call them the shops. If they looked at you you used to say I'm booked. We had to go out with them to be searched for anything: pins in our hair, matches or cigarettes or anything tucked down your neck. They used to search you all the way down — you couldn't get out of it and then they used to say you can go. If they kept anyone back, you used to say 'Now what the heck has she got on her'.

Respite from war work.
Land Army girls relax by the Victoria suspension bridge

I had a near escape once. We were all in the canteen at break — we had gone over onto the Powder 'cause they had shut the other down — and we were having a cigarette. I don't know from that day to this why I came out of the canteen with a lighted cigarette in my mouth. The police came running over.

'What's the matter?'

'You've got your fag, look!'

There was a drain by the side of me as it happened and I pushed it straight down the drain.

'Where is the cigarette?' he said.

'Down the drain', I said. 'There, you can see it. I'll get it up if you want it'.

Anyway nothing come of it thank goodness. I could have been in trouble. It was in case the wind blew 'cause it could have ended up near the powder. They had a perfect right. I was in the wrong.

My father was dead against us smoking. He always said: 'If you were supposed to smoke, you girls, you'd have a chimney on top of your heads'. He always smoked 'Willie Woodbines'.

We were allowed to buy cigarettes at a cheap rate and send them to the boys in the forces to boost their morale. Nobody realised just what a dreadful effect it had on the lungs. My husband smoked quite heavily during the war. When he came home he was smoking and when he died everyone was

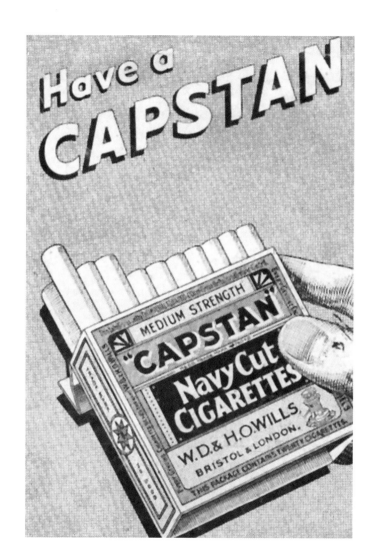

very shocked. I used to smoke but it was more of a social thing. I never really enjoyed it, but it was the thing to do. They weren't allowed to smoke in the factory.

My father used to be a sheep and cattle dealer but when the war came he went to work at the factory and he worked in the contraband. You weren't allowed to take cigarettes, matches or anything like that into the factory so there was this little building where you left all the contraband. He would look after them. That's where my father was: it was the first regular wage my father had ever had.

Falling Sick

People knew who worked in the munitions because their hair was a different colour.

Women — and men — risked and lost their lives making munitions. But the materials themselves were dangerous.

I was in Empty Shell where they cleaned the shells. They came in all greasy and horrible and they had to be washed out. You had to go down with a light to make sure there was nothing inside. I was out there for about six weeks because I was yellow and that. Didn't get jaundice exactly, but I lost all my periods and they were a bit worried I think. I mean everybody's hair went yellow. Terrible. Today it wouldn't be allowed.

I had to go over on the North Section, work on the cordite, which I said I hated. I knew that I couldn't do anything about it, and I had cordite poisoning. I was off work for 13 weeks. It made you sick. I couldn't keep water or nothing down, could I? I was in bed for four weeks. You had sick pay. When I went back they didn't put me in the cordite.

There was one lady there. I remember she was ill. She was crying. She didn't like it. Two of us helped her. I don't know whether she was distressed or what. You had to help one another out, didn't ya?

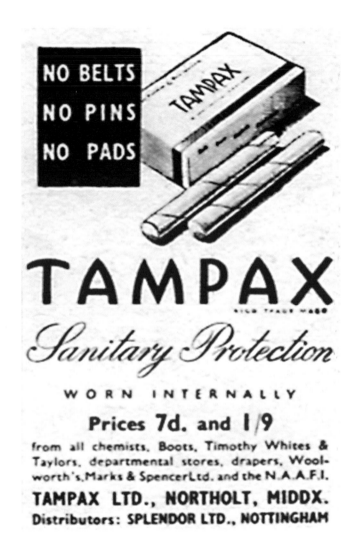
I got paint poisoning! I became very ill and then yellow jaundiced. All my life since my health has suffered — still at 78 I am still alive.

They were so short of TNT in the early stages of the war that they were using a lot of Austrian TNT, which contained a lot of foreign objects such as nails and screws. It wasn't safe to use until it had been inspected. They opened up one building with a conveyor belt in and these boxes of this Austrian TNT were emptied onto the conveyor belt, and a bloke on each side with a wooden stick spread it and picked out such things as bent nails. Well the chaps which were doing that started to go blue from inhaling this TNT powder stuff. One chap died. A friend of mine who was put on the job had sense enough to keep the floor wet, which made the atmosphere heavy, and you didn't get the dust, the stuff flying everywhere. But that was one casualty.

My mother worked down there in the First World War. Women's skin changed colour becoming yellow from an explosive powder called picric, so much so that they were called Canary Girls. Picric was later discarded.

You had to have several pairs of flannels, 'cause the TNT used to turn them dark blue. It used to ruin your blooming trousers.

They could have got TNT poisoning from the stuff we used to fill. There was one girl died from it. They used to have this stuff and it was liquid *gypo*, they used to call it. And somebody had to stand over this steaming pot and stir it. She was a big woman about 6 foot tall and rather plump. She was doing that and she got poisoned and it killed her, but they kept it quiet.

I used to get bad stomachs. I think it was when I used to get over tired with all the working and travelling. I used to go to the doctor and he used to give me a ticket for about two to three weeks. It was very tiring; you could do it for so long then you would get run down.

Your hair was yellow. Course you had a cap on. Anyway it comes alright after. It's the powder you see?

When I first went there, I chummed up with a girl who had been drafted from Hastings. We had to watch them clock out to go for their meal break, so by the time we went for our meal it was a kind of free for all. This person, who was called Molly, used to keep me a seat by her. Molly had only been there six weeks when she was taken very ill. She swelled up and was as yellow as can be. She had TNT poisoning. She was rushed into the general hospital. They said she couldn't go back there to work. The government trained her as a telephonist instead.

My aunt Jessy and my mother Emily were filling these very large bombs, when my aunt fell smack bang into the middle of one of them. They had to pull her out! Aunt Jessy had an allergy from the bombs on her face. It was like eczema. Her skin was never like that 'till she started filling these bombs.

Doris Hayes, Eve Lichfield and Jean McGaw outside Red Hill Hostel in the 1940s

When you got in to doing the powder your skin used to change colour. It used to go brown and your hair used to go ginger and all your clothes. It used to go right through your clothes to your skin. Our mam used to say we had to keep the same things for work: she used to wash and boil it, but it was still brown. They used to wash the overalls. You'd think: Am I ever going to be white again?

You could get different things wrong with you like a jaundice, but you were a deeper colour than a jaundice. That was when we were working in the Powder.

I wasn't very well at one time and they gave me six weeks or two months out of the Powder 'cause you were allowed a break out of it when you been in it so long. There was a doctor there that examined you and they weren't very keen taking you out of the Fill, you know. There was so many not been very well at one time. You went such a bad colour. I was real ginger when I finished there. My hair.

I packed up down at Rotherwas because I got the rash. You used to scratch yourself to pieces. They'd come round to see you when you were at home to examine you. If you'd had the rash and been

scratching it a lot you were no good to them then. That's when I finished and went to Redhill hostel to work. I used to go around the tables clearing up but if we were on 'till 11 I used to have to wash the dining room floor, to make sure there was no powder or anything. Things had to be just right 'cause the powder was a danger — we saw how it went that morning with that plane when it bombed the factory: just one hit and it's gone.

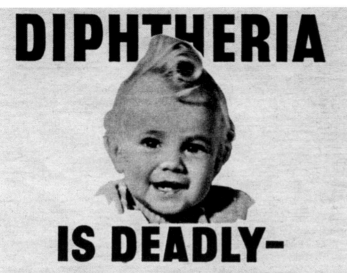

DIPHTHERIA IS DEADLY—

Give your child the protection medical science now offers. Read the facts below and apply at once to your Council Offices or Welfare Centre. Treatment is free.

IMMUNISATION IS THE SAFEGUARD

FACTS ABOUT DIPHTHERIA

Over 50,000 cases occur yearly in Great Britain. Between 2,000 and 3,000 of these die.

Even the best-cared-for child can get Diphtheria—it is not due to dirt or drains—and there are no "safe" areas.

Diphtheria is one of the worst dangers to children. It is particularly deadly to children under six years of age

Even when not fatal, it may leave ill effects which last a lifetime.

FACTS ABOUT IMMUNISATION

There is nothing to be feared from immunisation. It is SAFE and simple. Merely a "pin prick" which is over and forgotten in a moment. If an immunised child gets Diphtheria it is usually in a mild form. Immunisation gives almost certain protection against death from Diphtheria. Only two treatments are necessary. The best time is soon after the first birthday. Protection takes three months to develop so get your child treated NOW, ready for the Winter.

Issued by the Ministry of Health & the Central Council for Health Education

D2/1

Babies

I was pregnant while I was down there but I was alright.

I left when I was expecting my eldest daughter. Once they knew I was expecting, I went in to the checking of the boxes and the numbers that was going out with all the bombs. I didn't have to do any lifting or anything like that.

I did, I think, around five years on Hereford munitions. I left to have a baby anyway, which we never intended to have! She was a big mistake!

My boy was born at home just because it was the thing to have your children at home. When the second one came along, I had him in a nursing home in Southbank Road, but unfortunately I lost that one.

Pregnant women were allowed to work up until about four months, but anybody with any sense wouldn't have worked there when they were pregnant. You were breathing that stuff. Some of them would work, but I think it was better out of it.

I went to the doctor and he said: 'You've got to pack this powder business up'. I was about four months pregnant. So they didn't stop immediately you were pregnant. I went on — being sick in the morning and fainting. I had to finish in the end. I was beginning to feel ropey, you know, and I thought this wasn't any good. But it was a awful job to leave. You had to get a doctor's certificate and declare when your baby was due and … oh, it was still difficult to leave. I expect I should have seen it out if I hadn't have been pregnant.

I left at a certain time 'cause of the baby, like, not for her to go yellow or anything. You know, it was no good staying. I suppose it was no more dangerous than any other place, really. It was just ammunitions for the war and that was it.

Before I started at the factory I was 17 and I had a little boy. My mother looked after him.

I hated it at the factory. They emphasised to us how important it was. They would say: 'Think of the boys on the front line! They can't do without the shells and bombs'. Well, what could you? You had to go in. Anyway I was married in the March and the following March I had my first baby. I was down there 12 months. I was on nights and the baby was on the way so I packed it up. It was about the only reason you could pack up.

IN TROUBLE
"*I am only 16 and am expecting a baby; I am an illegitimate child, which makes it worse. My father has been very unkind to me lately as he seems to suspect something. Can you tell me where to go?*"

YOU poor child, you don't seem to have had much chance to learn honourable behaviour, do you? I am terribly sorry you have got yourself into this mess but try to make it a turning point in your life. Write at once to Miss Chapman, 117 Piccadilly, London, W.1, and do what she advises you; she will tell you where to go and you

I hated it down Rotherwas. My husband said: 'Well if you don't stick it, you'll have to go in the army, the air force or the land army'.

'Oh no', I said.

'Well, we'll have to have a baby', he said. So we went in for a baby. In those days, I'm not ashamed to say, I was a virgin. When I was married I was a virgin which they can't say now can they?

Whilst I was in labour the young doctor said to me: 'I've only ever seen another lady with those brown marks on her. And, he said, she was nice looking as well!' I thought he was a bit of a wolf, actually. I was laying there and they make me put me legs on me shoulders — so embarrassed! And after my son was born the brown marks went. They went after he was born. I often I wonder if it was the cordite, you know.

You didn't talk about Sex

I got friendly with a girl. She lived at Kington and she had to travel 20 miles to work. She was only about 5 foot but she was quite well built. I felt sorry for her because she was looking after her mother. We got very pally and we used to go down for about 7.15 a.m. to have a warm up. It was cold in November and December. We used to stand against the radiators to have a warm and then the Charge Hand would call you to your line so you didn't miss a minute.

Well this happened this one morning and she didn't come up to the bench. I looked round and she was still there so I popped across. 'Are you all right?'

'I don't know'.

'You should tell our Charge Hand'.

Later the Charge Hand said to me: 'Do you know what's wrong with her this morning?'

'No. She won't tell me what's wrong'. I couldn't go up because you dare not leave your bench. If you wanted to go and spend a penny you had to say where you were going.

Anyway the Charge Hand said to me: 'I think you had better take her up to the surgery. I'll carry on and do your job'.

I took her up to the surgery. There was a nurse and another lady there so I left her there. 'I'll come up in my lunch half hour'.

When I got back this nurse went for me. She went mad at me. She said: 'Your friend wasn't fit to walk up here!'

I didn't know anything about sex! You didn't talk about it. She was a big girl and filled her coat out—I never thought anything about it. I didn't know there was a baby there. We were all so innocent in those days. The nurse said: 'She has been rushed into hospital. You should know better at your age!'

I thought: 'What is she talking about?—Should know better?' Anyway she told me: 'There is a baby on the way'.

She had the baby on the way to the hospital in the ambulance. I went down the General to see her. She was in an isolation ward, right down the back. She had puerperal fever. I'd never heard of that. I was really in the dark. I wasn't allowed to go into that ward. I could look at her through the window. I went on the Saturday afternoon. I took her some fruit. I thought: 'Well her poor old mother won't be able to get in'. I used to feel sorry for her and I took her a few other little things and next thing I knew she'd died.

I can't believe that medical we had, because she must have had that baby within a month of that. Now what sort of medical was it? You had to strip to your waist and it was embarrassing. You covered yourself up as best you could. Why wasn't it picked up at those medicals? I don't why we had those medicals. Maybe the doctor was having a good time. I think the factory doctor was down St. Owen Street, at Wargrave House. Of course he's gone now.

Poor girl. What she must have gone through. Mind you it happened. When I worked at the camp, this other girl who worked at the top end, her baby had been born in the ambulance. Another one well built: you didn't realise if they were pregnant. We were so innocent in those days.

They were all so innocent then. You were threatened that if you kissed a boy you'd have a baby! Sex was never mentioned.

I started to get educated down there because some of them were really common. There was one girl, she came from the College Estate and every other word was a swear word. I wasn't used to it! I always wanted to be a nanny but they couldn't afford to let me go.

An unknown couple from the First World War.
He is wearing his munitions worker badge and armband

When we went down there everybody had to have a medical and you had to strip off, right to your waist. I didn't like that very much.

You had to have a medical and if they passed you fit that was it. There were about three or four doctors and nurses. As long as you passed your medical and you could bend your fingers that was alright.

We had several babies born. We had the Canadians stationed next door. The Canadians were responsible for that. If they were pregnant, they were dismissed then, you see.

I remember one morning, they came and said: 'Sergeant Major, there's a baby in the lavatory in the S block'. I couldn't believe it, but there was. In the bowl. Of course it was dead, the poor little devil. It was a lovely little boy too. With the one who had had the baby in the

DEAR LEONORA EYLES.
"I know all about birth control methods and have three children; I am doing a double job, factory work and looking after the children, and another child would be disastrous. We have no religious feeling against birth control but wonder if it is ethically right."

I CAN'T pretend to answer that question, my dear, but I can tell you what I personally think and my opinion is based on a good bit of scientific medical study as well as sociology. If you let Nature have her way, she will use you to produce more children than you can afford. Another baby, at the moment, would incapacitate you, temporarily at least, from doing your bit for the war effort which will make the world safer for your present family; if you and your husband try to keep apart you will be putting an unfair strain on both of you. You must sort out those arguments for yourself, as I cannot be your conscience, can I?

Looking for my Mum

I was born in January 1943, but brought up in Belgium. I thought I had been born in South Wales and only found out I was adopted when I asked for my birth certificate in order to get all my papers ready to get married. I saw the birth certificate and saw that my 'mother', Phyllis Mabel Probert, was not mentioned as my mother. I started to ask her questions about the past. It was only then that she revealed that I was adopted and that I wasn't born in South Wales as I had always thought, but in Hereford.

Phyllis, however, never revealed anything further about the adoption and only after her death did I begin the search for my birth mother. I discovered she was called Margaret or Peggy Clark, that she came from Scotland and that she had worked at the Rotherwas Munitions Factory — where my step-mother had also worked.

I believe I have now found my mother, but she still does not want any contact and I respect her wishes on that. Instead we have been busy trying to put together my background, going back to my grandmother, but so far we are only getting the information one word at a time. All I know for sure is that Peggy definitely is my mother, according to my newly found brother, Ken. I sent him some pictures of myself from when I was in my late 30s and early 40s. He was overwhelmed by the resemblance. He kept on saying: 'That is our Mum', but it was me — with my daughter and granddaughter.

Thelma Verhulst, searching for her munitions mother

HERE goes a poor woman who always was tired,
SHE lived in a house where help wasn't hired
THE last words she said were "Dear friends, I am going
WHERE washing ain't wanted, nor sweeping nor sewing
AND everything there is exact to my wishes
FOR where folk don't eat, there's no washing of dishes,
DON'T mourn for me now, don't mourn for me never,
I'M going to do nothing forever and ever"

lavatory while I was there, I was blamed for it. I had to go to court. I had to go and explain what had happened. I said I didn't know anything, didn't even know she was pregnant. She was a cook, you see, she used to wear an overall and a greatcoat. I could never tell. So they brought in 'inattention at birth'. That was the verdict that they brought up for the baby that was found dead in the lavatory.

They used to go to the doctor once a month for what they called 'free from infection' on their hands to see if they got any rash between their fingers. And the girl had seen the doctor and he didn't say anything. So that was the sad thing about a poor little baby.

There was a clock went missing one day. So then it comes home time and there was always these police on the gates checking as you went out. Anyway these police jumped onto the bus and said to this woman: 'What's that lump there?'

'I'm pregnant', she said.

'Would you like to come with me?' one policeman said. Because the men weren't allowed to touch the women. Anyway there was a police woman there and they asked her to undo her coat and there was the clock wrapped up in a roll-a-towel!

Good Times, Bad Times

We had good times and bad times.

I'm 91! It's so long ago, it's a job to remember what our feelings were. Surprising how much did go on as normal during the war.

The first night I was due on work, we couldn't get through on the Straight Mile because it was flooded. We had to go down Watery Lane and hop onto the railway and get in the factory through the railway, those who took the trouble to do so.

Two Land Army girls sample Herefordshire's traditional beverage — cider

When we had terrific floods down the Holme Lacy Road, there was a chappie who lived at Jays Hostel in Bullingham. We watched this man; he scratched his head, took his jacket off and his shoes and his trousers. He put them all on the fence and he swam up the Holme Lacy Road. That was something funny wasn't it? Don't know who he was! We all clapped him. Happy days.

There was the water at the bridge. They dropped us off the buses and they had put some planks of wood for us to walk on. There were these soldiers offering to carry anybody across the water. This one fellow said to this girl: 'I'll carry you over'. So he picked her up and started carrying her across and they both started laughing and fell in the water! This one chap wanted to carry me and I said: 'No thanks'. I walked through the water.

On the farm you were doing all sorts of things, stacking the corn, doing everything pretty well you know, hay making, everything. There were animals, but I didn't work with the animals, just worked more or less on the land. 'Tatoes, everything. Everybody liked working on the land. If I was on nights at the factory, I'd come home in the morning and I'd go out with my mum.

Farming was hard in those days. They didn't make money on the farm, like everybody said they did. We had the pigs and cows and a pony for the trap. When I came home from leave, they used to meet me at Leominster station with Peggy in the trap. A nice round thing with seats all round. Lovely. Very comfortable too. And one day, we only had a donkey. Imagine that! And all the kids kept saying 'Ee-aww!' all the way down.

Mother worked hard, making butter and scrubbing floors. We didn't have hot water or electric. We had oil lamps, and candles. I was glad that I didn't have to stay on the farm. I didn't like mucking out. And I was afraid of the animals. Well mum was afraid of the animals. So, I suppose, if she was afraid of things it made me afraid.

Dad tried to get me to milk a cow one day and that frightened me. Oooh, I didn't like the feel of it. Then he stuck me on a horse's back, and that scared the living daylights out of me as well. He did try to make me interested.

He had words with the boss. Mum told her what to do with her job, then they sent us up to Anglesey, for two or three months, my brother and I. When we came back they were living in Hafod Road, sharing a house with an aunty.

We had a search light battery here. Stuck there, it was terrible for the soldiers. Course they wanted to know all about village life. That was before I got married anyway. They had billets here and the lady that lived in this house did their washing for them and darned their socks. She cared for them quite a bit. I think there was some money attached to it.

Father was in charge of the Home Guard platoon. Then, because we had a phone, all those men had to be contacted, so I used to go round the villages telling them that there was a meeting at Preston Hall, at such and such a time and such and such a day.

At Stockley Hill somebody reckoned there was something signalling when planes were going over. I know they went, but I don't think the Home Guard found anybody.

If you were married to a serviceman you were allowed his leave off. If you were engaged to a serviceman you were allowed half that time off. I was working in a shop and I used to sneak the time off when my fiancé came home on leave.

Accommodation in Hereford was in short supply. Land Army girl Jean McGaw stands outside the temporary camp that was eventually replaced by Red Hill Hostel

I left school at 14. Out at work two days after my 14th birthday. And guess who I had to work with? Freddy Bulmer. I was his little girl in the office. And every day he used to say: 'I want you to come round the factory with me'. He had a stick, 'cause he was an old man, well he seemed a very old man to me. He used to have his hand on my shoulder.

But I did want to be a nurse so I went to Thornbury Hospital near Bristol. My boyfriend was a pork butcher in the market. All the Hereford girls used to be after him — he was so handsome. But he couldn't do without me and one day I was sitting on the hospital wall on my two hours off duty when I saw him: 'What you doing here?'

'I miss you', he said.

'Oh I miss you!' He grabbed me, took me to the matron.

'No, I can't let you go in case you elope', she said. 'Not unless you go to the police station in Hereford when you get back'. Which I did.

Life was so much more romantic then than what it is now.

We had a nice wedding. I remember seeing my wedding dress. There was a shop in Eign Gate called Walters and it was in this window — 'It's me, it's me', you know? But I hadn't got any money. We really saved up for it and it was still there, luckily. I had three bridesmaids. It was a big wedding for wartime.

We had to save up very hard because everything was on coupons you see. We had the wedding meal at home, you couldn't afford to go out — made your own trifle the night before. My late sister-in-law, she made the sandwiches and we had it at home. We didn't go away as a honeymoon but we did go to Evesham to his brother's house.

I married. He'd been married before, and he didn't think it was any good staying in Hereford because it would have been difficult for me, being the second one. In those days being divorced and then re-marrying was not done. I was the scarlet woman!

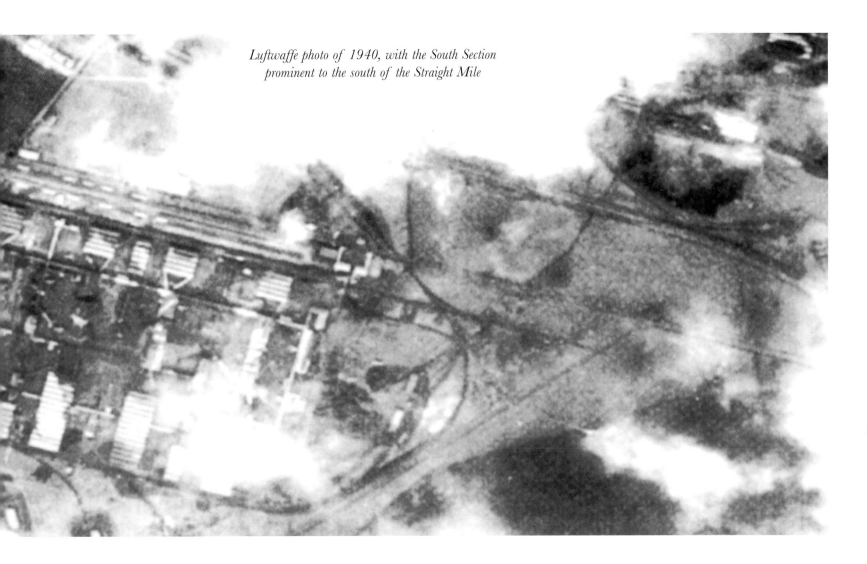

Luftwaffe photo of 1940, with the South Section prominent to the south of the Straight Mile

They were nice people from the Forest of Dean. Well there was this one girl and she was from the Forest and there was this man, he used to wear lots of gold rings making believe he was rich. He talked this girl into going with him and he reckoned he had this nice house. When she got there it was a caravan in a field and he locked her in this caravan when he came to work. I looked for her on the Monday morning and nobody knew where she was. She had nothing, only a bit of food. She had a nail file and she used this to scratch at the wood and eventually made a hole big enough to get through and she ran across the fields screaming, and a lady who lived near rescued her. You had to watch yourself — there was a lot like that about.

I was in the millinery department, I sold hats and bonnets, things that came down like a bucket over your head mostly! Older ladies, they always wore big black silk hats. Oh we kept them all in a cupboard and we used to have to brush them every week.

There was no family Christmas you know. None of the forces came home for Christmas. But I can honestly say Christmas passed so quickly those years. The factory was open so you were lucky if you were on a shift pattern where you were home on Christmas Day.

My husband was in the Royal Tank Corps and he went right through the war and was wounded in El Alamein. They sent me a letter from the War Office, stating that he was missing, presumed killed. Then about three days later I received a letter from him, to say that he was in Cairo hospital. They found his kit bag and all the letters that he'd written to me and that I'd written to him and they were all burned. And I had to write back to the War Office to tell them that he was in Cairo hospital. He recovered.

In 1939 I was 13 and all the street lights lamps went out. I said to my father: 'Oh dad how long is this going to last?' He said: 'Until this lot is over'.

Walking alone in the black-out, many a time I've been followed. Don't take any notice. It was alright if it was moon-light but if it wasn't sometimes they'd put the searchlights up, training on the planes. Then, all of a sudden, they'd all go out. And you know what it's like when the light goes out suddenly: it's black. Many a time I've bumped into a brick wall or pillar and said: 'Sorry'. To purchase a torch was very nearly impossible. They all took No. 8 batteries and you couldn't get them.

La Trine

I had to escape from France. There were about 400 A.T.S. stationed in France. They were driving all the ambulances. Wonderful girls they were too. They worked very hard. We never lost anybody. Nobody was killed. I was stationed in Nantes when the Germans came and we just walked out and left everything.

There was one kid on the river with her boyfriend, so the officer had to wait for her to come back up. They were very good, the officers then in those days.

We left all our uniforms and our rations and we just got on the first train we could. The French didn't help in the beginning. We wanted to get onto the train at Nantes and they wouldn't let us. However, when it was dark, we went up the sidings and got on the train when they didn't see us. But we didn't know where we were going. As we passed a big camp, and it said B.E.F. camp and one word said Latrine. So one of our kids ran down and said: 'I know where we're going! We're going to La Trine'.

The train went to St. Malo. And the last boat, the *Princess Astrid*, brought us home to Southampton. That was our escape from France.

Our parents were very relieved of course. They didn't know where we were, what we were doing or anything you see. And we were told you mustn't tell anybody where you are, where you're going, so we had to keep very quiet.

We had no street lamps until well after the war finished. I think everybody turned out to see the street lamps turned back on.

We had to have black-outs. You had a job to get black-out material. What they did advise people to do was get a wooden frame to fit in your window and draw your normal curtains on top of that. I remember my mother getting told off: 'Put that light out!' It was a candle!

Dad, my husband and my brother, they dug the Anderson shelter in the ground. It had just a seat to sit on as far as I can remember. I know we used to take candles down in clay pots to keep us warm. But people didn't bother. They never experienced anything, or else it would have put the fear of God into them.

Some had Anderson shelters which you had to bury in the garden. We didn't. We had a Table shelter. It was a steel table and you had to get under there if the air raid siren went. It was kept in the dining room.

The 9th Royal Berks used that barracks in Harold Street and the old regimental sergeant used to get them out in the back lane and to put them through square bashing. Oh the language! I didn't know what it meant. He effed and blinded, poor lads.

Brought up in Park Street, Hereford, Joan Hiles would watch the soldiers practise street fighting outside her front door

They used to practise street fighting. We had a laburnum bush in the front garden between the window and the front door. It was nothing to open the door to go to work in the morning and there'd be a squaddie behind this bush with a fixed bayonet. 'It's all right miss, I shan't hurt you'.

At the beginning of the war the Herefords were congregated at the old T.A. barracks. They were billeted on people in Park Street what had the room for them. There were some very nice people amongst them. Some used to come over the wall and help my dad dig the garden. They'd buy something to send home, but they'd nowhere to pack it so my mother said: 'Well come round and pack it at my house'. They'd come round and pack their parcels and write their letters.

And we had the Suffolks and the Lincolns. Of course the King came and inspected the Lincolns because they were being shipped. Less than half of them came back. I think they went east, that was before D Day. Of course they were not allowed to tell you. 'Careless talk costs lives. Walls have ears'. When I had a letter from my fiancé, it had been censored. Blue pencil straight through it.

Somewhere To Live

With so many new people in Hereford, finding somewhere to live was a continual problem.

The accommodation was so bad. I was sent to several addresses and they couldn't take me in. When one of the drivers heard of this he said come to me and my wife will look after you: and there was two firemen and myself in one bedroom! They were on different turns — when one was getting up, one was going to bed! It was murder because there were no railway houses here. The council wouldn't house us because we didn't have enough points.

I went to the town hall several times. I asked the Housing Manager, he was a nasty piece, if he couldn't he get me in somewhere. He said: 'You work on the railway and the railway people should find accommodation for you people'. I said: .Don't talk so silly!' We got crossed swords over it and I went back down the list quite a long way I think.

We moved to this cottage down the Holme Lacy Road. I remember the old chappie in the neighbouring cottage. His name was Piggy Williams. He used to have pigs. I was always over there doing things for him. My late mother-in-law, she came to stay with us one weekend. She lived at Whitecross. She came down crying.

'I'll never come down here to stay again!'

'Why mum?'

'I've just seen that wicked old man'.

You could hear these pigs screaming. He cut their throats with a knife and they bleed you see. Their meat is whiter they say. I never had her to visit with me again.

We had a bucket toilet right up the orchard, through the garden. If you got taken short, oh my gosh! I went to the

Colin Keats lived at Foxley Camp as a child. 'The Council modified our living room so that it could be used as a rent office. One of the staff used to come for the day, once a week, to collect the rents!'

council. I complained and they came down to see it and they looked at the cottage. There was a crack up the wall, just underneath the bedroom window on the main road. They said it would have to be condemned because of all the wartime traffic.

We'd been at Foxley Camp for about four years. I think the council had difficulty getting their rent so they asked us would we allow a rent man to have a day out here. Our front room was a very long room and it was breeze blocks so one of the neighbours and I decided we would paper them. We

Life at Foxley Camp for Colin Keats

spent hours cutting up newspapers and covering it to make it smooth then we put some pretty paper on. It looked quite nice. Our rent was 16 shillings a week and they reduced it to eight if we had the rent man in there once a week. They opened a window in our living room to collect the rents.

Our son passed for High School, but we couldn't afford to have kept him there on railway wages so I went out to work. Seven in the morning 'till 4 for just under £5 a week.

It was 1940. I worked in Chadds in Hereford and I had to go do something for the war effort. So of course I went down to the ammunition factory then. When my husband came home we managed to get a little flat at the hostel up at Ross Road. You know, you wouldn't think they were lovely now, but to us they were lovely.

Many stayed at Red Hill Hostel. They used to have some very good concerts there.

Red Hill Hostel and those flat topped houses over Hunderton, they were put up for the workers.

One night the sirens went and as they got cellars in the old houses in Park Street, we went down the cellar, and stayed down there. There was a special gas mask for a baby. You had to have a gas mask. The children used to carry them in a square box with a string round their neck.

Evacuee schoolchildren arriving in Hereford. Many were homesick; many others returned after the war to settle here

We had to have an evacuee. She was working. She'd be about 18. It was compulsory to have them if you got the room.

At Kidderminster we worked on aeroplanes in a tunnel. Working in Kidderminster was fine, because it had more machinery. Hereford never had as much machinery. It was a nice happy atmosphere up there. We had a lovely hostel. There used to be Queenie, Ruby, Elsie, Vera, Evelyn, myself. There used to be a little old man and he used to be keen on my friend Nancy. He always left her a little bouquet of flowers. She used to say: 'Oh Mary, you see what he's done again?' We used to laugh about it, poor old Nancy. She wasn't allowed to take them in to the factory, so we used to hide them or give them to the guard. We all done nights. We'd finish on Saturday morning at 8 a.m., catch the bus into Kidderminster and then catch the train back. We wouldn't have to go back until Monday.

At the weekends we would go dancing. We'd go up to the Kings Head for a couple of drinks and then to the Drill Hall, dancing till 12 at night. Then back home. We enjoyed it. It was relaxation.

Something To Eat

You got used to it, and we didn't starve you know. Well there's not all these modified foods like there is now you see? There wasn't the variety. But I mean, we got by. Mother was a very good cook. She was a cook in service, up at Holmer.

Even to wash up we used to get what they call a soap saver. It's like a wire basket on a stem, and you had to swish it about in the water to get your soapsuds.

The rations were really bad. I remember queuing in Eign Street one day. Queued for ages for some bananas. First time we had seen bananas in the war and they were pink! It was rationed you see: 2 oz. of butter, 2 oz. of cheese.

We had chickens, but my husband would never kill any of our chickens. Biddy our oldest chicken, she had died peacefully underneath the car — we had a car then. But he used to go rabbiting. He would kill rabbits and sell them for one and thrupence.

He was at the butchers in the market. They used to be open till 9 on a Saturday. I used to meet him, when we were courting, very smart, you know. He came down there with a parcel under his arm. Four trotters and half a pound of chitling! Not flowers, not chocolates: four pigs' feet and half pound of chitling! I used to love it.

We used to get a piece of meat, roast it on Sunday, have it on Monday and then you would mince it to make a cottage pie on the Tuesday. That's how it would go you see.

THERE'S MORE THAN ONE WAY TO COOK A RABBIT...

IF you keep rabbits, or you're lucky enough to get one now and then, you must send for the new Stork Leaflet No. 41. It's full of excellent recipes for cooking rabbit in different ways. Small families who can't finish a rabbit at one sitting will find the leaflet specially useful, for it explains how to make rabbit left-overs into a delicious curry, fricassee, a tasty broth, and so on. Every recipe has been approved by the Ministry of Food, so send for your free copy with the coupon below.

STORK MARGARINE COOKERY SERVICE

We used to go fishing all night, eeling on the Lugg Meadows. Skin it, clean it and fry it. Both of us did the vegetables. My husband, for his kidney beans, he used to put all his old woolly jumpers in the bean trench. He used to have beautiful kidney beans.

Damsons, plums, apples, pears, we had everything. I've got a damson tree up here now. Every third year is good for damsons. But we just give it away mostly. People were so generous — much more friendly in the wartime, I felt. We were happy.

Often I used to come home from a night shift at the factory, and go and stand in the queue at the butchers with my mum. And I mean the queues were long, they really were you know. We had rabbit and we used to eat pigeon. Pigeon is lovely, really lovely. My mum used to dress them and all.

We had workers' playtime in our break and basic meals which we were all glad to take because everything was very short. We were lucky in the country if you had a few hens, a few eggs. Still a lot of people kept a pig, you know; they had a killing. Country people were better off than the town I reckon.

Over 'ere and Over Sexed

American GIs in High Town on VE Day. (Photo: Tony Williams)

We used to go picnicking outside Hereford by the river some-where, and we met up with some Americans there, doctors and nurses. They were at Foxley, cause that was an American army hospital. They were quite pally, we met them a few times. My son was only a toddler at the time so it was must have been just as the war was ending. They used to bring us chocolates and all that sort of thing, and there was a big hollow tree there where they used to put all these things for us. And they wrote a little note to mother when they were finally finished.

I went to work at the American Red Cross (where Barclays Bank is now in Broad Street.) It was full of Americans. They were stationed at Foxley and this was their sort of night club-cum-restaurant, somewhere to spend the time when they were here.

Well I never had a thing off them, not a pair of tights. I remember once we were invited to a dance. I went with the girls and I had my wedding dress piped with red velvet to make it look like an evening dress. You couldn't afford an evening dress: there weren't any charity shops in those days. My friend and I were the only two in long dresses and a couple of Americans went by and said: 'Oh, they're officers' material'! We came straight home. We didn't like that.

When the Americans was in the town, my sister and I, we used to iron their suits out at my mum's, 'cause they liked soap up the inside of their creases you know. She and I,

OUR AMERICANS

It takes two to quarrel — it also takes two to make friends

where they were billeted outside opposite my mother's, we'd go up there at night, around the bonfire and we'd have pota-toes. When the officers used to come we girls would go and hide, and then, when they'd gone, we'd come back! We did have fun, clean fun though, no sticky business.

I had to open the American Red Cross up. My bicycle was punctured so my husband said: 'You'll have to have mine'.

'I can't get on a man's bike'. I was a very dainty, petite little thing you know? So he put me on it, give me a push and

I went up the road and then I thought 'well how am I going to get off this bike?' I got to Broad Street and there were all the Yanks outside waiting for me to open the door and I was saying: 'I can't get off the bike!'

So they said: 'Turn around and come back down and ride your bike into us'.

So that was how I got off my bike. It was laughable. Fell into the GIs' arms on the bike. Oh happy days!

Then the Yanks came, they were a darn nuisance. One of them asked me to the pictures and I said: 'Yes if my friend Maureen can come'. We went and he fell asleep in the cinema so we left him in there. He never spoke to us again. You can see the funny side of things now.

It was bad times and good but we got through.

We went to visit this friend one day and there were all these things, you know, hanging on the fence that the Americans had used.

This soldier stopped and he said to me: 'Do you know what the time is?' and I told him. He was on a bike and he come riding alongside me and he put his arm around my shoulder and he said: 'Where are you going?'

I said: 'I'm going home'.

'You don't want to go home, yet', he said and he tried to get fresh with me so I pushed him and he fell off the bike. There was some people walking up in front of me and I ran up and said: 'Can I walk with you please? That American there was trying to get fresh with me'. So if I saw an American, I was gone! I couldn't stand them!

Mind you, they got more money than our boys did. And their uniform was nicer. They had a nice, green serge. Very posh to what our lads had with that rough old khaki. So the girls preferred the Americans any day, because they had the money anyway to take them out.

They had some Canadians came over, and they were nice. I used to live by the cinema and they used to get in a group and sing in harmony and it was beautiful to hear! They used to sing 'On the Banks of the Wabush Far away'. You could cry! Listening to them singing with the melody.

I went into Wakefield Knights. I didn't stick it for long. I was supposed to do my apprenticeship there but I couldn't stick it. I went then to Kings, the London House — Etams now. I was there until I was 18, in 1944. Of course when I was 16 I was called to register. I was interviewed by the top notch of the W.V.S. which was Peggy Greenland and two others. And they asked where I worked, how old was I? They drafted me in to do voluntary work at the W.M.C.A. forces' canteen.

I was there then Thursday evenings from 7 o'clock until 10.30. I'd go and work on a Saturday if they were busy. I'd go work on a Sunday. I've even worked on Christmas Day and Boxing Day, and Christmas Eve so I put in a few hours. I've still got my badge.

In the canteen they were the soldiers, sailors, airmen, A.T.S., W.A.F.s, Land army girls. We also had French freedom fighters. But I will never forget when the Yanks came over. Coloureds as well. Coloured boys were at the barracks for a time. We were serving when two little coloureds came in and they looked so lost.

'Can I serve you?'

They looked at me and they looked at one another.

'Tea, coffee, sandwiches?'

So I called the shift leader and I said I can't make these kids understand. I want to serve them with their tea or coffee. I don't know what they want. And she said: 'What's the matter lads?'

And they said: 'She can't serve us'.

'Why not?'

'She's white'.

'Oh no we haven't got any of that here', she said. They were waiting for a coloured girl to come on and serve them! And with that two white Yanks came in.

'Hi honey, I want so and so'.

'I beg your pardon?'

'I want so and so'.

'Hang on a minute'. I said. 'You get behind there and wait your turn. Those two lads were here before you'. We didn't know what colour bar was!

'Oh it doesn't matter about that', said the Yanks.

'Now hang on', I said. 'Either you wait your turn or you found the door to come in so you can find it to go out, because I can refuse to serve you'. And I added: 'They can't sack me, because I don't get paid for this job. Take it or leave it'.

I was having none of that! I couldn't stand the Yanks. I couldn't get on with them. They were under the impression that they were the answer to every woman's prayer! And it didn't go down very well because they used to belittle our boys. That's where the saying came from: 'Over 'ere, over paid and over sexed'.

When you weren't on counter duty you'd get 'What time do you finish?'

'None of your business'.

'Can I see you home?'

'No you can not. My boyfriend's meeting me'. He wasn't of course.

Do you know what one young Yank said to me? He said: 'I only wish our girls was loyal to us as what you girls over here are to your fellows'. But we had far more courtesy from the coloured Yanks than we did the white ones.

There'd been a young man staring at me for weeks and weeks. He used to come in the Red Cross. He was French. And the doctor's wife said: 'He keeps looking at you'.

'Well I don't know him. I'm not interested. I'm married', I said.

She could speak a little French because she was little more educated, you know, and she said: 'Well he does like you'.

'I don't care, I'm married', I said.

Then my friend and I went to the Palladium cinema one night and a sign came on the screen: Would Mrs. XX — me — go to the foyer. I was wanted. It was him there with two GIs!

'What do you want?'

'He won't get in the jeep', they said. 'We have to deport him. He wants to look at you one more time!' So I had to walk with him to the jeep outside the Kemble Theatre and he just got in and drove off! And he gave me a note with his name on: Victor Demeuter and he lived at Po. He was a railway worker. He'd been captured or escaped or something and they were holding him there until they could take him back.

We often remember the day the Indian kissed my sister. The Indians were on the racecourse. They were turbaned,

Shadow on happiness

VD

Ignorance helps to spread V.D. The object of these advertisements is to tell the public how venereal diseases are caught and spread; and how they may be cured by early treatment.

What are the Venereal Diseases?
The main ones are Syphilis and Gonorrhœa, two different diseases caused by different germs. Syphilis is a killing disease. If not treated early and skilfully it can cause death or total disablement in early middle life. Unless an infected mother is treated early in pregnancy, she can pass on syphilis to her unborn child. Gonorrhœa may lead to chronic ill-health and inability to have children in both men and women.

How is V.D. caught?
In adults, almost always through sexual intercourse with a person already infected. The passing of the disease in any other way is so uncommon that it need not be feared. Venereal disease can be cured if treated early by a specialist doctor; self-treatment is useless and may be disastrous. Anyone who has the slightest reason to suspect V.D. should seek skilled medical treatment **at once.**

Clean Living is the real safeguard

FREE CONFIDENTIAL ADVICE AND TREATMENT are available at clinics set up by County and County Borough Councils. (For addresses, see local posters.) Further information can be obtained IN CONFIDENCE from your local Council's Health Department, or by writing to the Medical Adviser, Central Council for Health Education, Tavistock Square, W.C.1. Please enclose a stamped addressed envelope.

Issued by the Ministry of Health and Central Council for Health Education (VD 45-7)

real Indians, you know. And my sister was going for a walk into town one day and apparently there was two of these Indians coming towards her. She never thought anything of

Elizabeth Godsell and Ada Wright with their bikes outside Red Hill Hostel. A favourite trick of airmen coming to the dances from RAF Madley was to 'borrow' a bike for the journey home

it. But when she approached them, the one broke away and he caught hold of my sister, put his arms around her and he gave her such a kiss on her face. She fled home and washed her face. She was very prim and proper, my sister was. She was really upset about it. I think he run away. He was just overcome.

The Indians were stationed on the race course. Under canvas. And it was in the winter and the horses was up there. We had winters in those days. Even the guzz'unders froze under the bed, that's how cold it was. I forget what other regiment was up there, but do you remember Basil Radford, the actor? He was under canvas up there in the army. He was brilliant. He used to come and take part in some of the plays at the County Theatre. It was the old Palladium, Berrington Street, the Bingo Hall now. Derek Sellburg, the repertory company was there all through the war. Somebody called Franklin owned it then.

The Yanks were up at Litley Court, and they were out at Foxley.

First of all I started off in Lewis Smith's linen shop in Commercial Road. Lewis Smith's chemist was on the corner and the Baby Linen shop was next door. That was where I saw all the troops coming back from Dunkirk. It was horrific. They were coming up from the station. Those as could walk had to walk and carry the ones that couldn't. There wasn't enough ambulances to go round. Some times you'd get a group of say 10, 25, may be 50. They came in dribs and drabs, soaked in oil, blood-stained, carrying the ones that couldn't walk. But they were never downhearted. We'd all rush out of the shop and call: 'Welcome home!'

Railways

You used to get different buses like from Leominster, Ledbury and all round Ross to take the workers home. And other than that there was the train. On the main Gloucester line they used to do about six services a day to Gloucester and back. Then we used to get the shunters. A lot of local people were working on them. They used to bring in different things and take these great big covered wagons out. Of course the trains used to go in along the front of the buildings, then they used to go all down the buildings taking stuff in and bringing

A Keir Stuart and Co Ltd. engine that was delivered new to the Rotherwas factory in 1916, shown here when sold as being surplus to requirements

stuff out of the buildings. They used to have great big lorries coming up and taking coal to the boiler house, but if you wanted to move bulky, heavy goods, the railway would have been the way to do it. It was nearly all done by the railways. Although it was a very busy factory we didn't have the traffic on the road in those days like we've got today.

I was made a fireman as a railman. I started cleaning the wheels as well, the spokes, all the boiler and all that. Oh, that was still done. A fireman maintains the steam so the driver can do his work. That's shovelling coal, but it's no mean job, like I mean, you just don't do that without thinking. You had what they called lighter up to light the thing up from start: a steam raiser, that's what they were, a lighter up and steam raiser.

Your job was to get it correct and tidy to go off to your depot and work your train. They used to have slats of wood all nailed together with paraffin waste in between. They'd throw a couple of those in, and then coal around it, and carry on from there. It took hours to get it right.

You had several rail yards here. You had one at Barton; Worcester Side is what they call Moorfield, and Barrs Court and down to Rotherwas — they had to have a trip going down there. You'd be bringing the loaded ones back out, taking the empty ones down. You wouldn't know it was munitions 'cause, I mean, you had open wagons wrapped with a sheet over.

I was at Barton, that was the freight depot. We booked on at 4 a.m. in the morning for the first trip and the train left Hereford Barton at 4.30 a.m. and we picked up traffic at Worcester sidings, then round to Barrs Court and picked up some more traffic and away to Rotherwas. We pulled in on their side of the railway because there was 'ours' and 'theirs'.

There was two trains a day; two a day going in and out, average between 50 and 60 wagons. I've brought 60 away from there, everything to do with the war effort.

We couldn't tell what was coming from Rotherwas because it was all in sealed vans and then sheeted wagons. We didn't know what it was. Nobody was supposed to talk about it. There were enemy agents all over the country trying to pick up news.

The Americans had a big depot with their own sidings at Moreton-on-Lugg, own points and everything. These two vanloads had come into Barrs Court and they were attached to my train and they had to be attached to our van and there was an armed guard with them and he didn't know what was in them. I asked and he said: 'Your guess is as good as mine, sonny'.

We'd just got past Ross-on-Wye and this guard said to me: 'Have you got a spoon?'

He brought this tin of peaches out — not a small tin; it was big and he put the peaches on the lid. I had a knife in my bag so I had the peaches with my knife. They were beautiful!

On the Americans ambulance trains there was always a meal for the guard. But it was traumatic because I saw some

Munitions were carried out of Rotherwas on the railways through stations such as Holme Lacy

The Lost Engine

My father joined the maintenance department at Rotherwas in 1942-43. One day an inventory was received from the Ministry of Defence stating details of large plant held at the factory with an impending inspection to be carried out a short time later. The inventory stated one railway steam engine when, alas, the factory had two. In order to comply with the inventory from the Ministry, railway lines were laid to the edge of a nearby disused gravel pit, already filled with water, the excess engine fired up, and driven into the pit where it sank, out of sight to the bottom — bureaucracy gone mad!

(Exactly where the engine may have been dumped has been the subject of much speculation. Suggestions have included a pit on the north side, which was conveniently close to the track, and a lake close to Rotherwas chapel. But while amateur divers have offered their services in the search for the engine and at least one railway enthusiast has promised to recover and restore the engine if it could be found, the little train may be lost for ever — the most common account is that the engine was run into a pond on the south side and the pond later filled in and turned into a sports ground.)

dreadful cases, limbs that were blown off and blood all over the place. You know, when you think about wars, what a terrible thing it is to think we men working our lives out to blow other people to pieces. That's what it meant.

Fog and falling snow — there's nothing worse for railwaymen. You've got no light, you've got to listen for the whistle all the time. You get various whistles for what you want the driver to do. That's how you work because you couldn't see him. Your lamp was no good in the black-out. The circumference of the lamp was about three inches. You had a little wick in the bottom: that's all the light you had in the guard's van except the light from the stove. You were in complete darkness! You wonder why we lose our eyesight.

War Weapons Week, Hereford 1944. The city's Sea Cadets re-enact the battle scene in which Midshipman Cornwell won the Victoria Cross, for a parade float

In Barton there was a terrific fog and the train engines were all steaming and blowing off. They were all leaking badly. Of course they weren't in the sheds long enough to have any repairs done to them — they were forced out because of the war and the controller said to me your train is second in the block. It was nothing to see three or four trains lined up on the up and the down, waiting for men to book on. I was going between the trucks: I didn't hear this pilot engine making a shunt. I had my bag on my shoulder and he knocked the bag off my shoulder and I went down. It knocked me down on the ground. That was a near escape from death.

There was one young shunter killed. The signal man shouted to him: he rushed out straight in front of the pilot engine. That was a foggy night. Cut him all to pieces. It was a shocking job.

The Railway had a Home Guard and they used to guard Rotherwas Bridge and all that. I done fire watching myself at Griffith and Hart, where the Bulmers' Laboratories are now. They were corn merchants. I mean that was your food. If that went up, I mean the bakery would be all gone. You'd be there during the hours of darkness and then you would probably go home and go to work.

Women working the trains during the war time, it didn't go down too well. They had two guards and a travelling porter. The travelling porter looked after the parcels that had to be loaded in the various vans — she was a good girl.

Accidents

We were ever so lucky there considering what that factory turned out. I mean it was all round us.

There were a number of accidents. From time to time you had some mishap which varied in amounts of damage done. But the worst one was when the machine which mixed the ammonium nitrate and the TNT, mixed them up: that had an explosion which killed several people. There was another occasion when a loaded shell fell off the truck when it was being transferred from the Filling Sheds where stuff was filled, to the transit area for dispatch. It must have been a faulty fuse, 'cause it fell off the truck, which was loading them, and the poor chap pushing the truck, he ran after it blew up. He ran some distance along the corridor before he fell. As far as I remember, he came from Colwall.

I was just clocking in when a fellow was pushing a truck down from the Fill. One 25 pound shell fell off. I think it killed him and others.

There were the usual things which happens every day, like people cutting their hands or something like that.

There was nothing much used in the way of tools, such as they were. Scoops and all that were made from gun metal, which is not supposed to spark. But I've seen it spark. In one process they had, called Filling Houses, the walls were 3 feet thick, and half a dozen of them, with a steel door, to contain any explosion in there. I was passing one day, and there was a terrific bang, which shook me, but didn't hurt. In theory it shouldn't have gone off. The shells were filled automatically by tubes coming down and when they pulled a lever, it made the tubes come down and the powder, or liquid, would go in and the steel door would come down in front automatically. Now, in theory, those shells, half a dozen in a rack, would be so placed that the plungers coming down with the powder couldn't explode it because it was gun metal.

There was one time when a shell went off. They used to put these shells on the tables. Well somehow or other they'd put too many shells on the table and one fell off and it exploded and killed this poor little man. All he kept saying before he died was: 'My poor little girl'. He had a little girl. He thought the world of her.

I was in Unit Two, on the line, when one of the shells went off on the truck. And actually the trucker then, whose name I think was Price, used to live on the Hope Mansel Road. I think he was hurt slightly, but it wasn't all that bad you know.

In Naval Bombs, I primered and fused it. I had one gauge for fusing, one for primering. You put the fuse on first and the primer on second. The I.N.L., the person who

VITAL FACTORY PUT OUT OF ACTION

THE machine shop of a plant on important Government work was gutted, 450 auto-lathes were destroyed, and vital production was held up for months as the result of a knock-out blow, scored not by a bomb but a cigarette end—just one of the 1,000 accidental fires that are helping the enemy every day. Everybody should make it a rule never to throw away a match or a cigarette end until they are certain it's out—really out.

You can't be too careful!

Issued by the Fire Offices' Committee as part of a National Campaign supported by Government Departments concerned.

checked the shells, he used to have to put in the gauge, like a bit of plug. It used to go down the bottom of the shell to make sure the primer was right in. He got it wedged in the shell and he started messing with it. I got frightened and told him to stop as he was going to blow us all up. So he put it in the middle of the table and used another gauge. When we went for our dinner break, I said to him:

'Take that down to the breakdown shop because don't forget it's dangerous — it's primered and fused'.

'Yes I will', he said.

But I'm afraid he didn't. He must have tampered with it. It must have blew up. They came and told us to stay in the canteen. They took some of the girls back in to the other sheds, but numbers 15, 16, 17 and 18 had to stay. And we never went back to work that day. When we went back to work we weren't allowed anywhere near number 16. It was all cordoned off. I was put in priming 25 pound cases, the bottom half of the 25 pound shells. Obviously he killed himself. It was a shame, because he was a nice chap and he was married with two children. It upset us all.

One woman behind me, she dropped two long ones right by my legs. It's a good job they weren't ready to go off: I'd have had no legs! There was trouble about that. They said she wasn't doing her job.

The first accident I remember was an explosion and that blew them through the roof. One chappie, his face was bad where they had to pull it and stitch it. And then we had the bombing. We were on afternoons then and I said: 'I don't know whether I'm going in or not'. I didn't want to anyway. But we decided to go and we were in there and we had a purple warning in the afternoon. It was horrible.

In the summer of 1944, it was very, very hot. Grandfather worked there. Mines had been left out in the sun. Someone noticed the bubbling tar coming out of one of these mines. Then all of a sudden the mine went off: 'The factory's gone up!'

We had the bombs go off Whitsun weekend. It was very hot and the sun was on these windows and it made these mines go off. I think there was four or five altogether. They came and told us to get out. We had to go up onto the road. I got up as far as the main road and this bomb went off. Blew my hat up in the air and I couldn't move. Then it was all raining down around me and I thought: 'I'll never get out of here. This is my lot!'

It struck my leg and I couldn't move. It was like girders that had been blown up with the blast. Anyway it stopped for a bit and I ran to shelter behind some sheds and then there was a load more blown up. There was a kind lady up Dinedor road making us all a cup of tea. So that was the best cup of tea I ever had in my life. After that we had to go and work on the North Side because they didn't open that section up again.

I remember hearing the explosion. It blew our attic door. And my mother-in-law, who lived in Arran Avenue, it cracked her ceiling right across. It did quite a lot of damage in town. It was a terrific explosion.

My brother, Vincent Carey, known as Nick, was evacuated from Guernsey with his wife and children in June 1940. The Germans were likely to arrive at any moment after the retreat from Dunkirk. He went to Hereford and was one of the five

Sabotage

When we were in Number 2 there used to be this thing along the top, a pulley to lift the mines with. Well, one time, we had this little man there and I looked up and saw him on this beam. Then he went.

Tom was going to load and when I looked up it was off the pulley, off at the top. That's what that little man had done — he'd taken it off!

I said: 'Don't pull, Tom, the crane's off'.

He said: 'It can't be'.

I said: 'It is. Come and look'.

He believed me then. He said if he'd have pulled that we would have all been blown up! It would have come down on the mine and made it go off. Well at first they couldn't find this little man, but eventually they did. He was inside for the duration. He wasn't an Englishman, he was a foreigner. I think the word is sabotage.

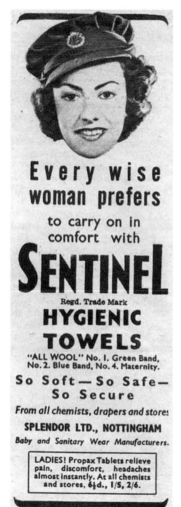

awarded the George Medal. My mother and I remained on the island. We heard the news on a forbidden wireless. When Nick died a few years ago his wife presented the medal to Guernsey Museum.

The bomb that blew up, they said it was a land mine. And the rumour was that this girl who was filling it rammed it too hard and it detonated. But whether that was the truth . . . I mean, we didn't get the truth.

You went down the long mile. There was a division between the North and the South. I went on the South to start off with, and then we did some time on the North where it's more navy stuff on the one side. Of course I think it were the North where the bomb went up. It completely gutted the one side of the factory, so you could tell it was a big bomb.

It was several hours before they really exploded. They thought they'd cleared the factory. My mum said: 'My God!' It was a biggest clap of thunder she had ever heard when that bomb went off. That's, what, nine miles away, look.

She said: 'Oh my God. I bet that's the munition explosion at Hereford'.

We were out. The shelters were full. They were all full. We were on the road. We were all crowded together in such a bunch and when it went up it, it lifted you up off your feet — you couldn't fight against it.

I mean we were hanging about for hours and when they got organised they got buses to bring us back home. We had a fortnight home. There was no work there until they got organised.

The biggest damage that was done, we had a great big bomb that wasn't sealed correct. That went up and exploded. It blew half the factory, it finished half the factory. It lifted some of us right through the air, off our feet, we were out. I had a huge big cut on my knee, which I had to go and get dressed. The mark is still there now.

We went a little bit out of the canteen, and just had a quick peep, you know. Shaken up, of course. One afternoon, there was a bit of a bang down there. Somebody saw chairs flying out from the place down there. Something had gone off, down there. It wasn't being bombed.

MINISTRY OF SUPPLY

SHELL MEX HOUSE,
STRAND,
LONDON, W.C.2.

28th September, 1944.

PERSONAL.

Dear Mr. Little,

I was very glad to hear from Miss Hallam that you had left hospital. I trust that while you have been at home you have made good progress towards complete recovery.

I am sure the Superintendent will be glad to see you back at the R.O.F. as soon as you are in a fit condition to return.

You may remember that I spoke to you and Mr. Tyler regarding official recognition of your gallant behaviour on May 30th, but as I explained, this matter cannot proceed quickly, though I can assure you that it is moving, and that in due course you and the others will receive recognition.

With kind regards,

Yours sincerely,

C. J. Robinson

D.G.F.F.

Mr. J.W.Little,
R.O.F. Hereford.

I must be truthful with you, we didn't spend a lot of time in the shelters, you know. The raids were all around us and when the siren went, you were supposed to go into the shelter. But in the end we didn't bother to go. I mean you were wasting time.

We lived in the Fireman's Quarters because dad was a fireman. The factory was one of the biggest in the country, but being in the middle of a filling factory, we never, never entered our heads to worry about it.

Then I was up the College Estate in the Girls Training Core, and we were marching up and down, and doing things up there. And then this explosion happened, shook the whole place. We couldn't go back home that night. I stayed with an aunt in Park Street and so did mum. And my brother stayed in Edgar Street with another auntie.

The explosion blew the windows and the doors in, in the Fireman's quarters. Bits of glass on the bed. It was a bit of a shambles. We had to patch that up a bit. But it could have been a lot worse.

Captain Overs, you used to see him go past to the offices. He was the boss. He lived under the railway bridge at the end of the Straight Mile, right inside there, on the right. It was up a bit of a bank, almost on the railway line. He had a little girl and a nanny. I used to go and baby-sit with her when her family went out. Poor child she pulled a fish kettle full of boiling water over herself. Nanny was blamed for the trouble.

She was scalded to death. She was only a toddler. The little girl was buried in Dinedor Church.

Quite a lot of people from Ross used to go by double decker bus when they cancelled us going on the train. One day on a windy day the double decker blew over coming back home by Harewood End. A few people had cuts and bruises, but nobody was really hurt.

We had a train from Leominster that brought the munition workers in. I think a lone raider followed the train and dropped a lot of the incendiaries, as you call them, along the track, but he didn't get our factory. Well it was just a fire along the railway track.

There were one or two surprise discharges. For what reason we didn't know. We could only surmise. We had no proof. One day they were there, the next day they weren't! The tale used to go round, 'Oh they've sacked old so-and-so, I wonder what he's been up to?' But things were very secretive, you see, the local papers and the national newspapers were not allowed to publish things during the war.

The Bombing — 27 July 1942

This particular Monday morning, apparently a German plane had followed the river up and I think it was lost and had bombs left on. So with that, he dropped them and blew up Empty Shell Two. If they'd hit Shell 4 we'd have all had it because that's where the shells were filled.

I had two aunts and they lived in Stonebow Road. Auntie Mary and Auntie Cath. This Sunday night my Auntie Cath said: 'Do you know Mary, I got a premonition'.

'What's she talking about?' Mary thought.

'We're going to go to work tonight and I'm not coming home tomorrow'.

'Don't be stupid!'

'I'll tell you what, we'll have a toss', she said. 'Heads we go to work, tales we don't'.

Turned out they went to heads, they went to work, but my Auntie Cath never came home.

Cath worked on Empty Shell Two. Auntie Mary was in charge of the canteen on the North side. We were there and we were on mornings as they were coming off. So we couldn't go in and as the plane came by the canteen — do you know what he done? He turned around and waved to the girls. And that was him going home then.

Cath was on the red shift and I was on the white. The white shift wasn't allowed to go in. Cath was in the area that got bombed. She used to have beautiful hair. It may sound daft, but she always had it neat and she had two rows of curls. When they found her, her hair was perfect, but her two cheekbones were blown out. She wasn't the only one. There was quite a few that worked there and was injured so they had to sort everything out and it took time. You couldn't do it in five minutes. Her friend, she was very seriously hurt. Cath died on the Monday morning and her friend died on the Friday.

We didn't know how she'd been hurt. All we knew was that she'd been found between 12 and 12.20 p.m. That was a long time because they'd bombed that before 6 o'clock. They said you couldn't get into the air raid shelter because the men had blocked it all off. They were protecting theirselves.

In Empty Shell they were allowed to wear jewellery. Cath had a beautiful gold watch — some very kind person took it off her wrist and kept it!

We didn't know who was hurt until my aunt in Hereford was notified. Then she got in touch with my aunt in Ross. That's how we found out. Anyhow she was buried in Ross churchyard. It was one of those things, unfortunate.

Well, we were just more or less finishing the night shift, and the lights went out. There should have been a big red light that shone right down the unit, but it didn't come on. So I dashed out of Dirty Way and I heard the sirens finishing. So of course I dashed back in. I said: 'All out, all out, sirens are going'.

We all started to race up this corridor, some of it was covered in. It was a boarded floor. And as we got up towards Number One, I happened to hear the plane, and I looked up and he was coming towards us. He was that low that I thought he was going to hit us. And yet I see the swastika on the side, then I see the pilot looking down at us with goggles on, and a helmet on, and in the distance I could feel these three bombs falling. They were coming down slant like.

A man shouted: 'Lie down, lie down, lie down', you know, like. What happened I don't know. Whether the blast knocked me out or what I don't know 'cause when I came to I was in the shelter with two young ladies you know.

'You're OK, you're OK', they said. I was frightened to death, I was. Honest. Tears were rolling down my face. And then the First Aid man come in and checked me over like you know. I was suffering from shock really, because they got a lot of casualties in you know.

I had no shoes on. 'Where's my shoes, where's my shoes?' And: 'Her's got no shoes on!'

I had heard afterwards that 11 had got killed. And I don't know how many got injured. Then the coaches was coming in with the other shifts on. They reloaded and took us home.

Very soon after the war began, a man named Bassett was the Principal Clerk. After the bombing, he asked me to go in with him, 'cause staff were not allowed to go into the danger area.

And, I went in with him and he was in tears. I picked up a corrugated sheet on the roadside to push it further back, and there was a girl's head under there.

It was surprising, what got damaged and what didn't. The central office block, the one that runs along the main road, they built an extension on the back. It had very secure doors on the building, but the bomb explosion blew two teak doors, the entrance, to the far end of the building inside.

Ken Hursey's Story

We had a very happy life in the army. And after he retired my father joined the War Department constabulary and he was promoted to Chief Inspector of this factory, in charge of the police down here.

Of course it was very idyllic. I loved Hereford. Especially then. It was even quieter still. We lived on the outskirts of the perimeter fence, lovely old house. Originally it was an old pub or something. It had a cider mill

Ken Hursey

on the back of it. It was down the narrow lane towards Dinedor Woods. The farmer lived right under the hill and he used to deliver the milk on his horse and cart. It was a lovely setting. It had a nice big garden and big orchard at the back. Upstairs I should imagine there must have been servants' quarters.

It was a beautiful summer that year. My eldest brother was in the Air Force and my second brother was in the army. I was 16, so they would be 22 and 20. They were both boy entrants. My eldest brother was a mechanic when he joined and then, when the war started, he wanted to be a pilot so he was sent to Canada to train. My other brother, who had been in Gibraltar for three years, was home on his first leave.

My eldest brother's wife and her mum came down to stop with us for a week's holiday. So being as we had the visitors, my brother was in my bedroom, my older brother's wife and her mother were in the one bedroom and my mother and father were in the other bedroom. I was relegated to the cider mill at the back of the house.

And on this, the morning of 27 July when the raid took place, the siren had gone off. But in those days nobody took any notice out in the country. It was very early, before 6 o'clock in the morning.

I remember hearing the plane come over and I got out of bed and went to where I could look straight over the factory and there was this plane swinging round and coming directly up the line of the sheds. They were all in a line and almost directly in line with our house.

Vera and Ernest Hursey, the police superintendent at ROF Rotherwas

The bomb bay was open and then I saw the bombs come out. I think he dropped three bombs. The funny part about it is, although the first two exploded I can't remember any noise, any sound from them. You know, you just stand there transfixed and seeing this thing come and the place bursting and the flames going up.

And then I watched the third bomb come down. It came down right inside the roof of one of the big sheds and then came bouncing out through the big doors where the trains

The Hursey family. All but Ken (front right) died in the Second World War: father Ernest, mother Vera and brother Ronald were killed in the bombing raid. Ken's oldest brother, Ernest, died in action with the RAF

used to go in. They used to run the trains in to pick up all the shells and it bounced straight out of this big open door, bounced along the ground and it cleared the perimeter fence and bounced straight into the front of our house. And everything from that moment was dead still.

I just turned round to run down the stairs. I thought: 'I'm going to tell my mum and dad that the bomb's hit the house'. And, as I was half way down the stairs, it exploded. It was probably on a short timed fuse, you see, so it wouldn't go off too soon. Had it exploded on impact it would have gone off in the factory, but it didn't; it just came and bounced over the ground into the front of the house and of course then it exploded.

And after that all I remember is coming to and finding everything was dead still and dead quiet. You couldn't hear a sound. It was so quiet. I was buried under all the rubbish. I was still on the stairs, sideways on, and all the rubbish and brick and everything was on top of me. I tried to move, but I couldn't move. I shouted for my mum and dad as you naturally would do, but I couldn't get a sound out. I thought: 'Where are they? Where are they? They wouldn't leave me here'.

Then I heard somebody running down the lane. It was so quiet. Somebody says: 'Is anybody about?' and I shouted: 'Yes'.

He said: 'Wait'. I'm sure that was Mr. Goodwin who was the farmer up the road. And then eventually there were a lot of men down there, pushing and digging and

Ken's father, Ernest Hursey, at Rotherwas

shoving and they got a lot of the rubbish off me and I managed to move.

I knew they'd all been killed. It was obvious when they pulled me out. They just sat me still and I was looking round. There were curtains on the trees across the road. There was nothing, just a pile of rubble. Of course, it hit the front of the house and that's where they were sleeping you see. I'm sure it was only the thickness of the walls of the old building which stopped the blast from blowing me to kingdom come.

It's a tragedy, the fact that my brother was on his first leave from Gibraltar. And my eldest brother's wife was down there and her mother. You just can't believe it, you know the timing can be just like that. That was the sad part of it.

Then I went to hospital. I had no injuries, none whatso-ever. My uncle, my dad's eldest brother, took me off to live with him in Surrey. Then when I was just 17¼ in the March, I joined the navy.

The German was said to be just off loading. I think that was a bit of a myth. With these aircraft, there was only a limited amount of fuel. They wouldn't be sort of wandering around the countryside looking for somewhere to bomb. I got a feeling he was designated to come here and drop these bombs. I think he was shot down over the coast as he was going back to Germany. But I think the pilot survived.

It was, what shall I say, fate really. In more ways than one. My brother had just come back from Gibraltar on his first leave; we hadn't seen him for three years. Very sad.

My eldest brother, the one who was a pilot, he came back from his training and was

Ken's brother, Ernest, killed in an air raid over Germany

stationed somewhere down the south of England. He was flying Typhoons and they used to go out on low level raids across to Germany. He got shot down as well and killed. So once he'd gone the whole family had gone. Then there was only me.

So what I did to deserve that I don't know. Still there you are. There must have been a reason for it. I still haven't found out what the reason is to be honest. I haven't become a great leader or anything like that. But that's it, that's life.

People asked me if I hated the Germans for that. Well no, not really. You can't hate a man who's dropped his bombs inside a military target can you? He didn't drop his bombs indiscriminately. He dropped them in the factory and it was unfortunate that it must have hit a girder or something in there, to deflect it. I mean we were doing the same to them and they were doing the same to us. My brother was doing exactly the same thing. Innocent people got killed the same there as they were here.

My husband was farming up on Dinedor Hill and he rushed down, and helped to get the young man.

My grandfather, David Jenkins, was a Munitions Foreman. One of the two bombs hit the factory injuring David. He had been assisting the evacuation of people, mostly women and was entering the building again when a wall collapsed on him. He died the following day.

My mother worked at Rotherwas during the First World War and my sister during the Second. I never knew people were killed during the raid — parents kept the news from us I suppose. I remember a Sunday walk to see the wreckage.

The night shift were coming out. I don't know how many hundreds there would have been. And he sort of came low over them, and they sort of waved to him, and didn't realise they were waving to a German plane. And I think somebody said there were about 60 that were killed out of them.

I was dressing to go on the morning shift when I heard the bomber going over, and looked out of my bedroom window and saw it. It was very very low. The morning was very dull. Although it was past lighting up time, I think, I surmised the lights had been put on because it was past black-out time. The first explosion happened before I left home. The casualties could have been far worse than they were because it was the changeover of the shifts, from the night shift to the day shift.

The place must have shone up like a beacon because of the weather conditions, the fact that they'd taken the black-outs down, simply because the time said they could do so when actually, they should have been guided by the weather conditions. There was one bomb went through the roof of Number One shed, and didn't go off, because it was dropped from so low a height that it didn't have time to get onto its nose. It landed flat and bounced out of the roof of the shed and left a hole in it, and landed on the cottage in Watery Lane. I think the total casualties in the factory were about 17. I couldn't be certain of that figure.

Crewmen from RAF Madley. This proved the final flight for Thomas Pitts, right, the wireless operator, when the Halifax bomber crashed in Nottinghamshire on returning from a bombing raid

We were just going into work. It dropped on Empty Shells.

It was between 6 and half past in the morning. We were just going into work when the siren went. We didn't have no sort of air raid shelters, we had sort of brick-built places. Went in there. Gosh, it's a good job it did drop on Empty Shells or I wouldn't have been here today, because we were flung from one side of the thing to the other.

I was there still doing an office job on the South side when the lone plane came over. We had heard the alarms and didn't take much notice then we looked up and saw the cross and dived for cover into one of the air raid shelters.

They built a tower in front of the Fireman's Quarters with a Bren gun on top. Merchant navy men taught the Home Guard how to use it. When the attack came two Home Guard ran up the tower. But they could not get the ammunition because the major who had the key in his pocket was asleep in bed.

My husband was on nights and he hadn't come home. I was at the gate with my boy in my arms, worried. I saw a neighbour and I said: 'He hasn't come home yet'.

'Haven't you heard? A bomb has dropped on Rotherwas'.

He came home much later of course. He said about the bomb. They'd all been asked to stay behind to pick things up and whatever you know. The German plane had been bombing somewhere, whether Birmingham or wherever I

Thomas Pitts (right) with fellow crewmember whilst training at RAF Madley

don't know, and they had one bomb left and his last bomb was dropped here. That hit Rotherwas.

I just finished the night shift and we just took the wooden shutters down to get a bit of fresh air and I went outside. I thought: 'What's that droning going on?' and I looked and I thought: 'Oh my God!' I turned around and I shouted to the Charge Hand:

'They've just bombed the South side, an aeroplane just dropped two or three bombs. I think one has just hit our side, I don't think it's hit the shops but it just dropped a couple of bombs over on the South side.'

She walked up to me, the Charge Hand, and she slapped me across the face!

'What you do that for?' I said. 'Don't you dare do that to me.'

'You don't know what you're talking about,' she said.

The sirens were all going then. I said: 'Who could make up a story like that? You great big ninny, there's the aeroplane going back.'

He was that low you could see men in it. I said: 'He's dropped one here. I don't know if it's the shops or just the corridor he's hit but he's dropped some on the South side. There's all the sirens going now.'

It was the end of our shift, the incoming shift was already coming on and they'd stopped them.

My friend went up to the Charge Hand and said: 'Don't you dare lay your hands on her.'

She came unto me after and apologised. As if anyone would make up a story like that. It was just a couple of spare bombs he had you see.

We were coming from the night shift. I saw this plane go right over, cause it was quite low. My sister was a conductress on the buses and she saw the bombs drop. Of course when it went over we didn't realise it was a German aeroplane.

Three of the men awarded medals for their part in saving lives on the fateful day in 1944 when a mine exploded at the factory. Vincent Carey is in the centre

I see the plane going over in the morning. I was cleaning at Barton sheds. He was coming over Bulmers towards the factory. He was actually coming I should say from Birmingham way. Then somebody said: 'Well there's a swastika on it'.

I think it was actually shot down anyway. I don't think it got back to Germany.

The early morning shift were coming on and we were serving them in the canteen and suddenly we had the 'danger imminent' signal, you know, lights going 'danger imminent'. So of course we put the shutters up in the canteen and, a lot of us, we ran through the kitchen out to the door outside. We were running in all directions. And we were looking down the Straight Mile, which

was Rotherwas Straight Mile. We saw the plane coming up, but we thought it was one of our own. Until, luckily, it veered sort of, it didn't come straight, as we'd have had it. It veered like a little bit to the left, and we saw the bottom of it open, and the bombs dropping. Of course, it dropped on the policeman's house and killed them all to the one son.

But it was dreadful, and of course it went up, up around, and by this time of course when that happened we were running in all directions, all of us going anywhere, you know, I ducked out through a door, and a man was squat down by a wall. I squat behind him, you know, because it came back over again. But of course it had no more bombs, but it was pretty scary!

It was ever so frightening, when you

saw that coming out from the bottom of the plane! A bit of a shock, I tell you!

And every night that week, the siren went. And we had to go down the shelters. I loathed the air raid shelter. I didn't like being down there under the ground. We had to be there though until the all clear went of course. It was narrow.

We wondered afterwards, whether the plane followed the buses, saw the buses and followed them because you know there were no end of buses coming in to the factory, bringing the workers in.

We were on nights and, before our shift ended, the siren went off. We all went out to the air raid shelter and we saw the plane going over. We guessed he was making it for the south 'cause he wasn't terrible high. We all scattered like heck and then, when it dropped, everything was delayed: we was late going home. And the later shift, which would been my mother and my sister-in-law, was later coming in. But they saw the plane 'cause we lived in Franchise Stone then like, and it was only a couple of miles out. There was a mess. Quite a few was killed.

Mr. Attlee came over to see where it was bombed and Gracie Fields came. It was a sad time of course. You think well, they're going to kill someone, but you know. You haven't got to think like that I suppose have you?

Civic Ceremony for those caught up in the 1944 explosion at the factory

We were sad for those that was lost like. We saw them coming out, those that could walk, and some was bleeding and some was . . . you know.

It was very upsetting. It was upsetting like, 'cause a lot of them had lost friends, or colleagues, and more than anything, their workmates. We didn't lose any like from our side, 'cause he passed over us. He must have known where he was going. He had that one bomb left to drop and that was it.

When it was all over like, we were just dumbstruck really. We heard the siren and we came out and we were

TOO BRAVE

"Three years ago I was injured in an air raid, and still feel dreadfully excitable and jumpy when the sirens go. I was in hospital a month, but refused to stay longer, as I wanted to get back to my job. I am not a person to moan or complain, but I admit I find it almost impossible to control my terror when I think of raids or hear gunfire."

YOU have probably been too brave. I know that sounds strange, but it is quite possible. A bit of moaning, or talking about such an experience, is a great safety valve. Will you let me write to you personally, and I will try to help you to get rid of such an experience and all the fears connected with it?

all rushing over to it as the aeroplane, and Jerry, went over. We weren't in there that long once it was dropped you see. We waited for the All Clear. I used to hate those sirens.

It's something you don't forget you know, when you're working down there. We only had that one air raid.

It was just that one off which killed people of course. How many, I'd forgotten, 'cause the lists used to be outside the town hall in those days. We used to go and have a look and then find probably that there was someone else added on.

We didn't know any names, we just knew some by sight. There was this one particular woman that my mate and I always spoke to and knew. And then we never saw her for a while, and we thought she had gone. Then this one particular day we saw her like, and we nearly died with shock! We were talking to her then.

'Oh gosh, we were so frightened. We thought you were killed'.

'No, I'm alright', she said.

Under Fire

1st March, 1945.

CONFIDENTIAL.

Sir,

The King will hold an Investiture at Buckingham Palace on Tuesday, the 13th March, 1945, at which your attendance is requested.

It is requested that you should be at the Palace not later than 10.15 o'clock a.m. (Doors open at 9.45 a.m.)

DRESS:—Service Dress; Morning Dress; Civil Defence Uniform or Dark Lounge Suit.

This letter should be produced by you on entering the Palace, as no further card of admission will be issued.

I am desired to inform you that you may be accompanied by two relations or friends to witness the Investiture, but I regret that owing to the limited accommodation available for spectators, it is not possible for this number to be increased. The spectators' tickets may be obtained on application to this Office and I have to ask you, therefore, to complete the enclosed form and return it to me immediately

I am, Sir,
Your obedient Servant,

Frederick James Tyler, Esq.,
G.M.

Secretary

Frederick Tyler's invitation to Buckingham Palace to receive his bravery award after an explosion at Rotherwas in May 1940

I did have a lot of experience of bombs dropping, of doodle-bugs, and the underground bombs and all sorts. I've seen houses that have been dropped down from the bombs, and one row of houses contained the wives and children of soldiers that were serving their country. They were all killed.

My husband was a corporal and I was expecting my second child. And we went on a picnic down by the docks, and then we heard this drove of planes going out. Then my husband said to me: 'There's one in trouble'.

So the next thing we seen this plane, a big bomber, and he was twirling around and around like that and then boof! It exploded, and that fell out in a little village not far from where we were.

Of course everyone in it was killed. But after the plane had dropped, you could hear the ammunition going off all the time. And it upset me so much that I was hysterical. Well I went to bed that night, and I woke up screaming. And Bernard, he was due to go back next day, but he wouldn't go, because he wasn't going to leave me like I was. So he was put in military prison. They kept him in there for three days. I used to go down and play cards with him and then they took him away. They wouldn't let me go and see him before they took him. And the next thing, they'd taken his stripes off him and that was that.

A surviving section of the factory left after a major explosion in May 1944

We were staying at Farnborough and I was living with Mr. and Mrs. Morgan. And Mr. Morgan, he was in the toilet and the blast blew him off the seat! And then another time I was out in the garden and I could see this plane coming in. I knew it was a different one to ours from the sound of it. And next thing, there was a line of washing out, about three doors away from where I was staying, and he came down and he peppered all the sheets with the machine gun. They brought

him down two miles out of Aldershot and then he was put on view. Sixpence to go and have a look at him!

Doodlebugs were planes, but there was no one in them. They would send them out with a light on the tail end. And if the light was all right, you were all right. But if the light went out, it just plomped like that. I was in hospital expecting my little boy and this doodlebug was coming, outside my ward. There was a chimney stack and this doodlebug was coming straight towards this stack. If it had hit this stack, it would have exploded our ward. It was coming straight and then it turned off and it went out and dropped two miles out on an empty cowshed.

I was sent to a private school just outside London and we had a bit of everything, high explosive bombs, parachute mines, doodlebugs and rockets as well. There was nothing much we could do about it. Only the funny feeling you got when you heard the engines. Their engines of the aircraft made a peculiar noise didn't they? You could tell which planes were friendly and which weren't by the engine noise, because Germans definitely had a certain note.

Perhaps you'd look out and you see they'd flooded the district with a lot of flares that floated down. A bit terrifying. You wondered what was coming next.

It did give you a funny feeling in the tummy when you knew things were coming. The siren went off and the people around where I was, they'd go scattering off to go down to the

Lily 'Fan' Forrester (right) from Belmont, Hereford, seen here after receiving her Royal reward at Buckingham Palace. Fan, born in 1901, was working as a charge hand at Rotherwas in the Second World War when a shell accidentally exploded in her section. She received a medal for her efforts in getting her section back to normal production by the following day. Fan explained that she wanted to get the munitions rolling again as quickly as possible — 'I was worried about our boys out there,' she said

shelter. I used to go out and watch all these amazing sights. And one old lady was coming out of her front door and the bomb dropped and a piece of shrapnel hit her there and she just dropped. She was killed instantly.

And then the street next door to us, there was an incendiary bomb. That dropped, but after it had dropped it was like as if nothing was happening. Then all of a sudden you'd hear this terrible rumbling and it would take all the houses down. It would go underneath and drop all the houses.

You used to have the whistling bombs. You'd hear this sort of whistling before they hit the ground. Terrible.

After a while you get immune to that. You know what's coming is coming and that's it. There's nothing you can do about it.

I stayed in London through the first lot of doodlebugs. Flying bombs and then they flew over the V2s. We had them all round us. Actually I think my husband and I heard the first flying bomb come over because it was late night and we were in bed. And we heard this thing coming over and then we heard an explosion. They were terrible things, 'cause if you were out walking and you could see one going over, you made for shelter. If the engine stopped that was it: they came straight down.

I wasn't very brave and yet I stuck it out. But once the big ones came over, they were land mines you see. They just demolished everything all round you. They were huge. I never stayed there long enough to see one. I'd scuttled home.

The day I came home, land mines were dropping. Apparently our train had just drawn out of the station. They heard that Paddington station had been bombed and my mother was absolutely terrified. I was coming down the Avenue — somebody shouted: 'Here she comes!'

I remember going for a walk once and seeing an unexploded bomb on the side of the road. They evidently defused it 'cause nobody had stopped going past it.

My son was at the High School and they had quite a bunch of shrapnel that I picked up in the streets around there. I remember sending a piece home to Hereford and it was goldy colour. I remember saying when I sent it home, this was the gold that London streets were paved with.

We were bombed at Ocle Pychard. He dropped the bombs all across the fields. It blew the farmhouses away and killed the bullocks.

The only bomb we had in Preston was when they jettisoned on the way home. Bredwardine had a couple of land mines didn't they? I know it rocked us. Oh lord I shall never ever forget it. My mum and dad thought it was in our fields and they got up with their Tilley lamp and they were searching. But it was just out of the village.

The first bomb that that I heard, I was in the boy scouts. And we were camping out at Upper Breinton. There were other scouts there from other places, like a jamboree. We had these bell heads at the time and in the middle of the night, a tent pole came straight down between meself and the lad called Joey Forrester. Never heard the bomb, but that's what it was.

VE Day

Food shortages caused by rationing were overcome for this VE Day street party in Church Street, Hereford when everyone clubbed together to lay on the feast

Are we the forgotten few?

It kept open after the war. It went over as a storage depot, with greatly reduced staff. People were sent back to their towns of origin, because they came from as far away as Scotland. Buses used to come in and load up to take them down to the station. There were a lot of tears amongst them.

VE day, that was when the war ended wasn't it? Everybody out in the streets with their flags and their tables of food and all the rest and dancing and everybody was having a good time. Oh it was a relief.

I was pregnant when he left so she didn't see him until she was three, but she knew him because I'd taught her his photo, you know, and when he came home and I said to her:

'Who's this then Val?'

Imperial Service Medal

Sir, I am commanded to forward the Imperial Service Medal which Her Majesty, the Queen, has been graciously pleased to award to you in recognition of the meritorious services which you have rendered.

I have the honour to be Sir, your obedient servant.

(One of the girls reading that said: 'You've got a title!' But the Imperial Service Medal was automatic, as long as you hadn't offended in some way. As long as you hadn't hit the foreman or something like that!)

'That's my daddy!'

He was really overjoyed. To think that she recognised him!

But then they said there were jobs waiting for them when they came home, but there wasn't. There was nothing waiting for them at all. He had a very hard time for quite a while after he came home. He had to go on to social security. And that was nothing at all, because we had to find the rent and all. It allowed us 7 shillings 6 pence a week, and out of that we had to buy food and pay the rent. So it was very, very hard times.

After the war, everything changed, because everybody was so poor, and they couldn't afford this or that. I always liked to dress pretty well, even years ago, and I couldn't get any stockings. So I bought this stuff and I painted my legs and I went out with my brother-in-law, with my little girl in the punt. He belonged to the fishing, angler's, whatever and it poured down raining! All this stuff was running down off my legs!

There was only me and my young brother from Dilwyn who went to the war. I'll tell you what did happen when I came home. We had this Welcome Home money. The villagers had collected so much for me and my young brother — £77 each. Wasn't that nice? I mean, £77 was a lot of money in those days. That's the three little villages had collected the money between them. And they were very poor, the villagers were, in

Mary Lewis (second right) was on the way to the pictures with her friend when they were 'kidnapped' for the celebrations.
'It was VE Day and my twentieth birthday'

those days. It went in my post office book. It's still there now. Everytime anyone gives me any money, I put it on my post office book and then I get the interest. It's grown, my little pot of gold! It's grown!

I would have liked to have said thanks for that money you gave us during the war.

When I was married, my auntie, she made me a victory V. She made it like with red white and blue paper, and I had it on the front of my dress with a horseshoe. I'm there with this V on my dress. I look a proper Charlie!

It was great. I mean you cry don't you really? You all have a good cry.

In 1945 at the end of war, everybody seemed to go to town. They were dancing round the street. People were shouting: 'The war is over. The war is finished. You can go home now!' We came up through the town and there were people going mad, shouting and waving flags.

There was a wonderful spirit during the war. A wonderful spirit, helping each other. It's never come back since. Everybody helped one another you know? But after the war finished, it all went back to normal. It was wonderful while it lasted. Odd, isn't it? In adversity, everybody sticks together. But once it's finished, everybody forgets. I suppose that's human nature.

THE CHILD HE HADN'T SEEN

Leave at last! Father is home again and this time, not only his wife but their child — their first — whom he's never seen, greet him with out-stretched arms.

How proud he is! Snapshots after all don't tell one much, but here's the finest and best baby in the world.

When natural feeding failed the doctor advised mother to get Cow & Gate Milk Food, and baby from that day never looked back!

Why not get COW & GATE for *your* baby today, and also have the pleasure of seeing the look of pride on your husband's face when on his return home he sees what your loving care and Cow & Gate have together achieved!

©

COW & GATE MILK FOOD
"Babies Love it!"

REMOVE BLACK PAINT WITH A CAUSTIC SOLUTION AND A LONG-HANDLED BRUSH.

YOU CAN SCRAPE OFF ANTI-SHATTER SOLUTION WITH AN OLD SAFETY-RAZOR BLADE.

MAKE AN ATTRACTIVE CHAIR COVER FROM BLACKOUT CURTAINS AND GAY SCRAPS OF CHINTZ APPLIQUÉD ON THE BACK. PIPE THE COVER WITH A BRIGHTLY COLOURED BIAS BINDING.

When the war ended, it was a completely different life, as you know. There was no cap and apron and 'yes mam; no mam'. The big houses had to take what cleaners they could get.

After the war ended we had to take these shells apart and take all the stuff out. I didn't like that so I didn't stop there long. One night I was late and I had to go and see, I think she was the labour lady, for being late and she started telling me off so I said: 'Can I have my cards in the morning?'

That was that. I'd had enough.

Eye Witness was funded by the Local Heritage Initiative which is a partnership between the Heritage Lottery Fund, Nationwide Building Society and the Countryside Agency. This book and the project recorded the recollections of former munitions workers like Nora Foster, seen here with Bobbie Blackwell (left) and Bill Laws (right). Almost a hundred people helped with the project

In Memoriam

September 1940: Three die and three others are injured in an explosion
September 1941: Three die and six others are injured in an explosion
July 1942: At least 17 are killed and 24 injured in a German bombing raid on the Factory
October 1942: Two die and four more injured in an explosion
May 1944: Two die and several are injured in the biggest explosion at the Factory

Amongst those killed at the factory were:

Frederick George Bull, 41, of 37 Locton Street, Bow, London. Injured at Royal Ordnance Factory. Died 26 October 1944.

Florence Carter, 47, of 14 Ladycroft Avenue, Hucknall, Nottinghamshire. Died at Moorlands, Watery Lane, Bullingham, 27 July 1942.

Ernest Henry Chesterman, 58, of Bridge House, Wye Bridge. Died at Royal Ordnance Factory, 27 July 1942.

Daniel James Reginald Davies, 36, of Notts Cottage, Old Road, Bromyard. Died at General Hospital, 27 July 1942.

Frederick James Dyke, 47, of 3 Henry Street, Ross-on-Wye. Died at Royal Ordnance Factory, 27 July 1942.

William Garland, 45, of The Lodge, Vennwood, Bodenham. Died at Royal Ordnance Factory, 27 July 1942.

Edwin Gwilliam, 38, of Yew Tree Cottage, Christchurch, Coleford, Gloucestershire. Died at Royal Ordnance Factory, 27 July 1942.

Bertha Hursey, 40, of Moorlands, Watery Lane, Lower Bullingham. Died at Moorlands, 27 July 1942.

Ernest James Hursey, 48, of Moorlands, Watery Lane, Lower Bullingham. Died at Moorlands, 27 July 1942.

Corporal P. Hursey, of Moorlands, Watery Lane, Lower Bullingham. Died at Moorlands, 27 July 1942.

Vera Hursey, 23, of 14 Ladycroft Avenue, Hucknall, Nottinghamshire. Died at Moorlands, Watery Lane, Bullingham, 27 July 1942.

David William Jenkins, 50, of 46 Belmont Avenue, Hereford. Injured at Royal Ordnance Factory, 27 July 1942. Died 28 July 1942.

Frederick Smith Raper, 41, of 31 Ants Nest, Church Street, Ledbury. Injured at Royal Ordnance Factory, 30 May 1944. Died 30 May 1944 General Hospital.

Beatrice Mary Saunders, 22, of Walkers House, Shelwick. Injured at Royal Ordnance Factory, 27 July 1942. Died 31 July 1942 General Hospital.

James John Shine, 33, of 5 Paynters Terrace, Merthyr Tydfil, Glamorgan. Died at Royal Ordnance Factory, 27 July 1942.

William Constantine Walton, 50, Special Constable, of The Residence, Kenchester. Died at Royal Ordnance Factory, 30 May 1944.

Kathleen Blanche Wheeler, 31, of 72 Stonebow Road, Hereford. Died at Royal Ordnance Factory, 27 July 1942.

Veteran Voices

Herefordshire Lore has been campaigning for additional names of workers to be added to the Rotherwas Memorial.

They include:
Annie Adams, Joan Adams, Elizabeth Allen (née Reece), Wilfred John Archer, Majorie Ballinger, Elsie May Brace, Louisa Harriet Brace, Sybil Bromage, Beatrice Maud Brookes, Vera Butler, Kathleen Carmichael, Dora Carpenter, Florence Clarke (née Wargen), Elsie Clayton, Kezia Clifford, Molly Clifford, Reuben Charles Davis, Annie May Davies, Bessie Amy Davies (née Welch), Edith Davies, William Thomas Davies, Eva Dew, Clohilda Dickinson, Winifred Fuller, Emily (Pam) Glover, Arthur Gregory, Violet Lilian Griffiths (née Williams), William and Norah Griffiths, Eddie Gwilliam, Marie Hill (née Wills), Mary Hill, Lily Hodges, Doreen Holbrook, Violet Nellie Hooper, George Howells, Catherine Jones, Edgar Jones, John Jones, James Langford, Kathleen Lawley (née Davies), Bertram Levett, Elsie Marsden (née Aspley), Cissie Mayne (née Aplin), Florence May Miles, Dorothy Morgan, Rosetta May Morris, Archibold Raymond Nicholls, Winifred Violet Nicholls, Clive and Vera Oakley, Bill Parker, Thomas and Dorothy Passmore, Marjorie Powell, Fred Preece, Grace Price (née Arrowsmith), Doris Prosser, William and Gladys Richard, Ivy Robson, Hannah Maria Royston, Beryl Sadler (née Davies), Phyllis Shipton, Dorothy Smart, Dora Stephens, Ruby Stephens, Gladys Thomas, Kitty Verrill, Anna Walker, James Wilkinson, Albert Wills, Cecil Thomas Williams. (Additional research: Faith Ford).

If you or a relative worked at ROF Rotherwas, please send us any details you can recall and the names of anyone who worked there, to Veteran Voices, c/o Herefordshire Lore, The Pavilion, Castle Green, Hereford HR1 2NH, or email info@herefordshirelore.org.uk.

Kezia Clifford, Arthur Gregory, Clohilda Dickinson, Gwen Caldicott, Kitty Hall, Dorothy Morgan, and Clive & Vera Oakley